MICHAEL TRENT

Legends of the Lawless: Pirates Vol. 2

Rise of the Buccaneers 1600 – 1700

Copyright © 2023 by Michael Trent

All rights reserved. No part of this publication may be reproduced, stored or transmitted in any form or by any means, electronic, mechanical, photocopying, recording, scanning, or otherwise without written permission from the publisher. It is illegal to copy this book, post it to a website, or distribute it by any other means without permission.

First edition

Contents

Introduction

Pirates, those enigmatic figures of the high seas, have perennially captured our collective imagination, weaving their tales into the intricate fabric of maritime history and folklore. The era known as the Age of the Buccaneers stands as a particularly riveting episode in this narrative. It was a time marked by audacious exploits, larger-than-life characters, and a remarkable blend of infamy and heroism. This exploration invites you on a journey into the lives, legends, and enduring impact of the most renowned pirates of the buccaneer period.

Our story unfolds in the Caribbean, the pulsating heart of buccaneer activities. A labyrinth of islands and secluded coves provided ideal hideouts for these sea-faring outlaws. The era's geopolitical dynamics further stoked the flames of piracy. European empires, locked in a perpetual struggle for dominance, often sanctioned privateers to raid enemy vessels and settlements. These privateers, sanctioned pirates in their own right, frequently veered into outright piracy, seduced by the allure of vast riches and unbridled liberty.

Among these tales, the saga of Henry Morgan, a Welsh privateer who turned to piracy, vividly illustrates the murky line between sanctioned maritime warfare and piracy. Morgan's most notorious exploit was the bold sacking of Panama City in 1671, a feat that brought him not just immense fortune but also legal complications. Remarkably, despite his piratical ventures, Morgan eventually became Sir Henry Morgan, knighted and appointed Lieutenant Governor of Jamaica, exemplifying the intricate interplay between piracy and political power.

The Age of the Buccaneers was also an era of significant technological and tactical advancements. Pirates pioneered a form of democratic governance, often electing their captains and making decisions collectively. They modified their ships for enhanced speed and agility, transforming them into fearsome predators of the oceans. The emblematic Jolly Roger, with its stark skull and crossbones, emerged as a symbol of this defiant ethos.

But the story of these buccaneers is not merely one of looting and brutality. It mirrors the specific socio-economic milieu of the era, where the boundaries between legal and illegal, allegiance and betrayal, were frequently ambiguous. The pirates were, in many respects, products of their time, navigating through the complex currents of colonial expansion, trade disputes, and societal structures.

Their legacy transcends the tales of buried treasure and fabled sea battles. These pirates challenged the social and political norms of their era, occasionally ascending to the status of folk heroes. They ignited a spirit of adventure and freedom that continues to resonate today, influencing literature, cinema, and popular culture. The archetypal pirate image – complete with a parrot, eye patch, and treasure map – remains a source of endless fascination and entertainment.

Delving deeper into the lives of these extraordinary individuals, we uncover narratives of ingenious tactics, remarkable voyages, and monumental conflicts. We peer into the personal dimensions of these pirates – their aspirations, fears, and the factors that steered them towards a life of piracy. Furthermore, we scrutinize their influence on maritime history and their role in shaping historical events.

The Age of the Buccaneers was an epoch of paradoxes, where acts of villainy coexisted with displays of bravery. It witnessed the rise and fall of some of history's most infamous pirates, leaving behind a legacy that still captivates the imagination. As we embark on this exploration through the golden era of piracy, we invite you to reacquaint yourself with these legendary figures, not merely as notorious outlaws of the seas but as intricate characters who played a significant role in the rich tapestry of maritime history.

Wang Zhi

Wang Zhi, a notable figure from She County of Huizhou, now part of modern Huangshan City in Anhui, China, had an intriguing familial background. His mother and father both shared similar surnames, Wāng and Wáng respectively, leading to some historical accounts referring to him as Wāng Zhi, instead of the more common Wáng Zhi. From an early age, Wang Zhi immersed himself in the thriving salt trade of Huizhou, a region revitalized by its direct access to the lucrative Ming government's salt monopoly. Despite his early success and accumulation of wealth in this trade, fate had other plans for Wang Zhi, as his business eventually crumbled, forcing him to seek new opportunities in the southern province of Guangdong alongside his associates Xu Weixue and Ye Zongman around 1540.

In Guangdong, Wang Zhi found himself in a less regulated environment, especially concerning maritime trade. This allowed him and his associates to construct impressive seaworthy junks, large enough to transport contraband items like saltpeter, silks, and cotton to markets in Southeast Asia and Japan. This period marked a significant turning point in his life, as he began to interact with Portuguese traders, who had established themselves in the region since their conquest of Malacca in 1511.

However, Wang Zhi's activities were not without controversy. At the time, the Ming dynasty had strictly prohibited all private sea trade, insisting that all maritime commerce be conducted through the "tribute trade." This system required foreign states to present tributes to the Chinese court, recognize themselves as vassals, and receive gifts in return, often viewed as humiliating by the foreign traders. The tribute trade was also insufficient for the growing market demands, both domestically and internationally, due to the Ming's stringent regulations on how often a vassal state could offer tribute. Wang Zhi's smuggling operations emerged as a response to these unfulfilled market needs, providing a much-needed supply to a demand that the official trade channels could not satisfy.

On the historic date of September 23, 1543, Wang Zhi embarked on a remarkable journey with Portuguese sailors to Tanegashima, a Japanese island southeast of Kyushu. This voyage was monumental, as it marked one of the first instances of Europeans setting foot in Japan. In Japanese historical accounts, Wang Zhi was referred to as Wufeng, and his scholarly background in Confucianism and ability to communicate with the Japanese using Chinese characters written in the sand played a crucial role in bridging cultural gaps. The common written script between China and Japan at that time facilitated this unique form of communication.

The arrival of the Portuguese with Wang Zhi caused an immense stir among the local population due to their unfamiliar appearance. Their presence quickly reached the ears of the island's ruler, Tanegashima Tokitaka. The young lord became particularly intrigued by the matchlocks carried by the Portuguese. Wang Zhi, with his linguistic skills and cultural knowledge, adeptly served as an interpreter, explaining the mechanics of these firearms to the fascinated lord. This event was the catalyst for a significant technological shift in Japan. The matchlocks were swiftly replicated, and their use proliferated throughout the country, significantly influencing the warfare dynamics of the Sengoku period. These firearms became known as tanegashima, a name derived from the island itself.

The introduction of these Portuguese matchlocks created an unprecedented demand for saltpeter, an essential component of gunpowder. Wang Zhi, ever the opportunist, was perfectly positioned to meet this demand. Japan, lacking domestic production of saltpeter, became reliant on imports. Wang Zhi capitalized on this by importing Chinese and Siamese saltpeter, while also exporting Japanese sulfur, another key ingredient in gunpowder, to Siam. This trade not only brought immense wealth to Wang Zhi but also solidified his reputation in Japan and among various foreign nations.

During this era, Japan was in the throes of a protracted civil war, and the absence of a strong central authority — neither the emperor nor the shōgun wielded significant power — provided Wang Zhi with the freedom to engage in patronage agreements with regional daimyōs, the true power holders of various territories. Initially, Wang Zhi established his base on Fukue Island, negotiating with the Uku clan, lords of the Gotō Islands, for settlement rights. This led to the formation of a thriving Chinatown near the Uku clan's castle. Moreover, Wang Zhi maintained a residence in Hirado, at the northwestern tip of Kyushu, under the patronage of the local lord Matsura Takanobu. Wang Zhi's presence in Hirado attracted not only other merchant-pirates but also the Portuguese, who began sending their "black ship" to Hirado almost annually, a practice that continued until the establishment of Nagasaki.

In 1544, a significant turn of events unfolded in Wang Zhi's life when he joined forces with the Xu brothers, leaders of a prominent pirate syndicate based in Shuangyu, Zhejiang. Originating from the same She County as Wang Zhi, the Xu brothers quickly recognized his adeptness and vast experience in trade. As a result, Wang Zhi rapidly ascended within their ranks, initially assuming the role of their financial supervisor. His expertise and leadership skills soon led to his promotion as the commander of their armed fleet and as a counselor on military affairs, earning him the esteemed title of Captain Wufeng.

Wang Zhi's established connections with Japan became a crucial asset for the Xu brothers. In the same year, a Japanese ship on an unofficial tribute mission to China made a stop at Tanegashima before arriving at the Chinese port city of Ningbo. Lacking the necessary official documents, the ship was rejected by Ningbo's officials. Wang Zhi, with his persuasive skills and strategic thinking, convinced the Japanese emissaries to divert and illicitly trade their goods in nearby Shuangyu instead. The following year, Wang Zhi guided more Japanese traders to Shuangyu and encouraged Xu Dong, the head of the Xu brothers, to initiate their own voyages to Japan. This strategic move transformed Shuangyu into the primary hub for illicit Japanese trade in China.

With the rapid growth of his enterprise, Wang Zhi began employing Japanese fighters to safeguard their cargo against rival pirates and the Ming navy. His strategy expanded to include defeating other pirates and absorbing their followers into his own growing consortium. The local residents of Shuangyu held Wang Zhi in high regard, as the lucrative smuggling trade brought unprecedented wealth to their island. Transitioning from subsistence agriculture and fishing, the villagers began manufacturing weapons and armor for Wang Zhi and his contemporaries, repurposing copper coins for ammunition, saltpeter for gunpowder, iron for swords and guns, and leather for armor. Their support for the pirates was so profound that they provided not only daily necessities but also offered women and pledged their own children to the cause, with many young locals eagerly joining Wang Zhi's ranks.

However, the Ming court strongly condemned the illicit trade and piratical activities centered in Shuangyu. In a dramatic turn of events on a stormy night in June 1548, the experienced general Zhu Wan led a fleet that devastated Shuangyu, filling its harbor with stones to render it permanently inoperable. Despite suffering heavy losses, Wang Zhi miraculously escaped the assault with the aid of the summer monsoon winds. Xu Dong fled overseas, leaving a power vacuum that Wang Zhi seamlessly filled, assuming control of the syndicate. His prior roles in controlling the fleet and treasury of the Xu brothers made his transition to leadership almost unopposed.

The obliteration of Shuangyu in 1548 marked a significant disruption in the established illegal trade network, resulting in the scattering of smugglers along the Chinese coast. Many, amid this chaos, turned to outright piracy.

Wang Zhi, however, remained undeterred. He swiftly repositioned himself at Ligang, located on Jintang Island, where he continued to grow and strengthen his consortium. Recognizing the strategic advantage of advanced weaponry, Wang Zhi adopted Mao Haifeng, a skilled trader from Zhejiang proficient in Portuguese cannonry, as his son. Utilizing Mao Haifeng's expertise, he equipped his fleet with formidable Portuguese cannons, bolstering his naval supremacy.

In 1551, Wang Zhi orchestrated a decisive move against his rival, Chen Sipan. Forming a coalition with other merchant-pirates and with the covert support of Ningbo military officials, he successfully defeated Chen Sipan. This victory not only cemented Wang Zhi's dominance in the China seas but also drew many pirates under his banner, to the point where it was said no ship dared to sail without displaying his insignia.

Attempting to navigate the complex political landscape, Wang Zhi sought to have the Ming government lift the maritime prohibition and legitimize his operations. He portrayed his expansion as an effort to maintain coastal peace, collaborating with Ming officials by surrendering Chen Sipan to them. However, his efforts were met with minimal recognition — a mere 100 shoulder-loads of rice. Feeling insulted, Wang Zhi defiantly dumped the rice into the sea and unleashed his pirate fleets along the Chinese coast in an act of retribution.

The Ming government, in response, deployed the military general Yu Dayou with a massive fleet in 1553, aiming to oust Wang Zhi from Ligang. Wang Zhi, adapting to the circumstances, fled to Japan, where he had previously established strongholds on the Gotō Islands and Hirado. In Japan, he proclaimed himself the King of Hui, adorning himself in royal colors and surrounded by standard-bearers, signifying his regal status. His influence in Japan was not limited to these islands; it extended to forging alliances with prominent clans like the Ōtomo of Bungo and the Ōuchi of Yamaguchi, and his associates even infiltrated the court of the Satsuma clan in Kagoshima.

Wang Zhi's strategy in Japan involved amalgamating desperados from across the region with his predominantly Chinese forces. He launched pirate fleets, known as wokou ("Japanese pirates"), to raid the Chinese mainland. These wokou raids, part of the Jiajing wokou raids, initially targeted coastal settlements for provisions and trade goods. However, the raids escalated in scale and ferocity, evolving into large-scale assaults capable of defeating garrisons and besieging cities, affecting regions from Korea to Guangdong and even threatening the secondary Ming capital, Nanjing.

While Wang Zhi maintained that he never personally led these raids, his objective seemed clear: to intimidate the Ming government into legalizing private overseas trade. Despite his claims, the Ming government held Wang Zhi responsible for the widespread devastation along the coast. The Jiajing Emperor, viewing Wang Zhi as the principal instigator of these upheavals, issued a decree for his capture, dead or alive, marking him as one of the most wanted men in the empire.

In July 1555, a significant shift occurred in the Ming dynasty's approach to handling the escalating wokou piracy crisis. Hu Zongxian, hailing from the same Huizhou region as Wang Zhi, was appointed to tackle the issue. Contrasting sharply with his hardline predecessors like Zhu Wan, Hu Zongxian adopted a more pragmatic approach, considering the liberalization of trade as a potential solution to the piracy problem. Recognizing the complexities of the situation, he sent envoys to Japan with a dual mission: to seek assistance from Japanese authorities and to directly negotiate with Wang Zhi, aiming to persuade him to surrender.

In a gesture of goodwill, and possibly as a strategic move, Hu Zongxian ordered the release of Wang Zhi's family from imprisonment. They were relocated to his headquarters in Hangzhou, where they were placed under his personal care and supervision. This act signaled Hu Zongxian's willingness to engage in diplomacy and his understanding of the personal stakes involved for Wang Zhi.

The meeting between Wang Zhi, Mao Haifeng, and Hu Zongxian's envoys took place on the Gotō Islands. Wang Zhi and Mao Haifeng expressed that no singular authority in Japan had the power to command the cessation of pirate activities. However, they were intrigued by the possibility of having their trade legalized. In exchange for a pardon of their crimes and permission to present tribute to the Ming court, they proposed actively combating other pirates.

Hu Zongxian conveyed this proposal to the imperial court in Beijing, which reacted with skepticism and indignation. The idea of Wang Zhi, a Chinese national, presenting tributes was perceived as having seditious undertones by the Ming government, as traditionally, only foreigners were allowed this privilege. Despite this, the court did not outright reject Wang Zhi's offer to fight the pirates and soon, Mao Haifeng began operations to eradicate pirate strongholds on Zhoushan Island.

Amid these negotiations, a complication arose. Wang Zhi revealed that Xu Hai, a key pirate leader within his consortium, was launching a raid on China, and Wang Zhi was unable to intercept him in time. This urgent development momentarily halted the peace efforts as Hu Zongxian redirected his focus to countering Xu Hai's raid in 1556. Remarkably, Xu Hai was taken aback upon learning of Wang Zhi's negotiations with Hu Zongxian, a revelation Hu Zongxian strategically used to his advantage. This psychological tactic led to Xu Hai betraying his allies, ultimately resulting in the quelling of the raid, with Xu Hai and other pirate leaders being killed. This pivotal event cleared the path for the resumption of negotiations between Wang Zhi and Hu Zongxian, marking a potential turning point in the longstanding battle against piracy in the region.

On October 17, 1557, a significant event unfolded as Wang Zhi, along with a substantial trading fleet sent by Ōtomo Sōrin, arrived at Cengang in Zhoushan Island. Ōtomo Sōrin, buoyed by the potential reopening of China-Japan trade, had high hopes for this venture. However, the arrival of this fleet sparked fear among local officials, who mistook it for another wokou invasion, prompting them to mobilize troops in preparation for a possible conflict.

Adding to the tense atmosphere, upon reaching Cengang, Wang Zhi became aware of a sinister plot. Lu Tang, a lieutenant of Hu Zongxian, had allegedly schemed to bribe Ōtomo's men to capture Wang Zhi. This revelation cast a shadow of doubt and suspicion over Hu Zongxian's true intentions, putting the merchant-pirates on high alert. To alleviate these tensions and demonstrate his commitment to peace, Hu Zongxian took the extraordinary step of sending a high-ranking official as a hostage to the pirates.

During these delicate negotiations, Wang Zhi presented his conditions for surrender. He demanded an imperial pardon, a naval commission, and the reopening of ports for trade. In exchange, he committed to patrolling the coast and using force if necessary to persuade other raiders to retreat to the islands. Hu Zongxian was prepared to advocate for Wang Zhi's requests to the throne, but the political landscape was rapidly shifting. Hu Zongxian's patron, Zhao Wenhua, a proponent of appeasement, had fallen from grace due to embezzlement charges. Additionally, rumors circulated that Hu Zongxian himself had accepted bribes from Wang Zhi and the Ōtomo to overlook their crimes. These allegations severely restricted Hu Zongxian's ability to petition for Wang Zhi's pardon.

Instead, Hu Zongxian advised Wang Zhi to direct his petition to Wang Bengu, an investigating censor known for his hardline stance, in Hangzhou. Confident and seemingly untouchable, Wang Zhi arrived in Hangzhou in December, where he was treated with respect by authorities wary of provoking his followers. During his stay, Hu Zongxian enlisted Wang Zhi's expertise to assist in the production of matchlocks for the Ming army, significantly influencing the widespread adoption of this weapon in China.

However, in February of the following year, the political tide turned irrevocably against Wang Zhi. Wang Bengu had him imprisoned, though he was afforded certain luxuries like books and healthy food, leading him to believe this was merely a temporary arrangement. This illusion was shattered on January 22, 1560, when an imperial edict pronounced his death sentence. On the day of his execution, Wang Zhi was brought to the execution grounds in a palanquin, realizing only then the gravity of his fate. In a poignant final moment, he called for his son, bestowed upon him a hairpin as a keepsake, and embraced him tearfully, lamenting, "Never have I imagined that I would be executed here!" He was then beheaded before a gathered crowd. In a tragic aftermath, his family was reduced to slavery.

The repercussions of Wang Zhi's execution were immediate and grim. Mao Haifeng, in a vengeful act, dismembered Hu Zongxian's hostage and abandoned any hope for peace. The wokou raids, unimpeded by Wang Zhi's demise, continued unabated until 1567.

Wang Zhi's legacy is a complex and contentious one, embodying both the persona of a pioneering merchant who advanced maritime trade and the infamy of a "pirate king" at the helm of a violent enterprise. His influence and actions cast long shadows, affecting political narratives and destinies long after his demise. Wang Zhi's name, synonymous with controversy, became a potent political weapon, used to tarnish and discredit opponents.

In 1562, several years following Wang Zhi's execution, Hu Zongxian, despite his attempts at negotiating with Wang Zhi, faced forced retirement. His downfall was partly attributed to accusations of leniency and alleged collusion with Wang Zhi, exacerbated by their shared regional origin. This incident highlighted the lingering stigma associated with Wang Zhi.

The political weaponization of Wang Zhi's legacy was further evident in a 1565 political purge. Xu Jie, targeting his rival Yan Song, implicated Yan Song's son, Yan Shifan, in a conspiracy to overthrow the dynasty in collusion with remnants of Wang Zhi's pirate faction. The outcome was grim; Yan Shifan was executed, and Hu Zongxian, caught up in the scandal, perished in prison.

Even historical events such as the Japanese invasions of Korea (1592-1598) were linked to Wang Zhi. The History of Ming suggested that Toyotomi Hideyoshi was emboldened to invade Korea and China by remnants of Wang Zhi's gang, who portrayed the Chinese as deeply fearful of the Japanese. This historical narrative cemented Wang Zhi's reputation in China as both a pirate and a traitor, with some branding him a "race traitor" (hanjian) for his collaboration with Japanese pirates.

Contrastingly, in Japan, Wang Zhi is remembered more favorably as a key figure in Sino-Japanese trade rather than piracy. In places like Fukue and Hirado, where he had significant influence, his association with trade is emphasized. Historical sites such as Chinese-style hexagonal wells from his era and a Chinese temple he frequented in Fukue have been preserved. In Hirado, Wang Zhi is celebrated for introducing the Portuguese and initiating the prosperous Nanban trade. His legacy is commemorated with a statue and a stone stele marking the location of his former mansion.

Sir John Hawkins

John Hawkins, hailing from a lineage of distinguished shipbuilders and naval captains, was born into the bustling naval community of Plymouth in Devon, England. His birthdate, shrouded in historical uncertainty, is estimated to be sometime between November 1532 and March 1533. The son of William Hawkins, a pioneering English mariner who first ventured to Brazil, and Joan Trelawny, the sole heiress of the Trelawny family from Brighton, Cornwall, John grew up amidst tales of the sea and exploration. His life was further enriched by his familial ties to Sir Francis Drake, his second cousin, who was raised in the same staunchly Protestant household.

John's life, however, was not without controversy. Before he reached the age of 20, he was involved in a fatal altercation with a local barber named White from Plymouth. The incident, resulting in White's death, was scrutinized by the coroner, who ultimately declared White the aggressor. Fortuitously, Hawkins's father's influence secured him a royal pardon for the incident.

Hawkins then joined forces with his elder brother, William Hawkins, in the realms of shipping and privateering, honing his skills in these lucrative maritime ventures. He is also believed to have provided services to the Spanish ambassadors during the negotiations for the marriage between Mary I of England and Philip II of Spain. Intriguingly, Hawkins often referred to King Philip II as "my old master," a testament to their complex relationship, and in Spain, he was known as Juan Aquines.

Around 1559, John Hawkins made a bold move. He ended his partnership with his brother, withdrawing a substantial sum of £10,000 from the business, and relocated to London. There, he married Katherine Gonson, the daughter of Benjamin Gonson, a notable figure in the Royal Navy administration. Together, they had a son, Richard Hawkins, born in 1562. The mystery of whether Katherine was Richard's biological mother or stepmother remains unresolved, as their marriage occurred after Richard's birth. Nonetheless, Richard's affectionate references to Katherine in his later years suggest she might indeed have been his birth mother.

John Hawkins' seafaring ventures before 1561 took him to the Canary Islands, a pivotal journey that exposed him to the harrowing realities of the Atlantic slave trade. It was here that Hawkins first learned about the lucrative but morally contentious business of capturing individuals from Guinea, along the African coast, and selling them into slavery in the Spanish Caribbean colonies. Recognizing both the risk and potential profit of such ventures, Hawkins meticulously formed a syndicate. This consortium included notable figures like Sir William Winter, Sir Lionel Duckett, Sir Thomas Lodge, and his father-in-law Benjamin Gonson. These men shared not only the financial burden but also the inherent risks of this perilous enterprise.

In 1562, Hawkins embarked on his maiden slave-trading voyage. Commanding a fleet of three ships - the Saloman, Jonas, and Swallow - he navigated down the African coast to Sierra Leone. There, in a dark chapter of his career, Hawkins captured and enslaved approximately 300 individuals, forcibly taking them from their homeland. With his human cargo, Hawkins then set sail for the Caribbean. Operating outside the bounds of legality, he had neither Spanish nor Portuguese permission to trade in their colonies. Nevertheless, Hawkins found a way to sell his enslaved captives in Isabella, Puerto de Plata, and Monte Christi. These were locations where local authorities turned a blind eye to government trade embargoes, allowing him to conduct his illicit business. In exchange for the enslaved individuals, Hawkins procured pearls, hides, and sugar, items highly valued in the European markets.

The success of this trade was so profound that upon his return to England, Hawkins received a disturbing yet telling honor from the College of Arms. He was granted a coat of arms depicting an enslaved man, a stark symbol of his involvement and profit from the inhumane slave trade. John Hawkins is widely regarded as the first English merchant to fully engage in the Triangle Trade. This infamous trade route involved exporting English goods to Africa, exchanging them for enslaved people, then selling these individuals in the Americas, and finally, transporting foreign goods back to England for sale.

John Hawkins, with a blend of charisma and strategic insight, successfully convinced Queen Elizabeth I to support his second venture into the slave trade. He not only secured the Queen's backing but also attracted investments from notable figures in her court, including Robert Dudley, the 1st Earl of Leicester, and Edward Clinton, the 1st Earl of Lincoln. William Cecil, the 1st Baron Burghley, played a supervisory role in this enterprise. In a significant gesture of royal endorsement, Queen Elizabeth granted Hawkins the use of one of her own ships, the formidable 700-ton Jesus of Lübeck, and permitted it to fly the Royal Standard, a symbol of her direct patronage.

On the 18th of October, 1564, Hawkins embarked from Plymouth on a fateful journey with a fleet of four vessels: the Jesus of Lübeck and three of his own ships. His actions on this voyage were a stark testament to the brutal nature of the slave trade. Hawkins captured over 400 individuals from Africa, some through transactions with the Portuguese, but many others through direct and violent raids along the African coast. His departure from Africa on the 29th of January, 1565, marked the beginning of a harrowing journey for these captives.

Hawkins' first stop in the New World was Borburata in Venezuela, where, despite prohibitions on trade, he cunningly executed a faux display of military force, in collusion with the local governor, to facilitate his dealings. His next destination was Rio de la Hacha, where he resorted to actual force to negotiate what he deemed 'fair' deals. There, he sold around 300 enslaved individuals, along with clothing, linen, and wine, receiving payment in gold, silver, and other precious commodities. Hawkins also secured commitments for future sales of enslaved people.

After completing these transactions, Hawkins set sail for England. In need of water, he navigated to Fort Caroline in Florida, a French colony. Discovering the French settlers in dire straits, he astutely traded his smallest ship and some provisions for cannon, powder, and shot, which the settlers no longer required as they prepared for their return to France. This exchange was pivotal, providing the French with the resources they needed to survive and plan their journey back home.

The voyage, steeped in moral ambiguity, was financially successful, yielding an astounding reported profit of 60%. Hawkins' return to England was marked not only by this financial gain but also by the introduction of two novel items to the English: the sweet potato and tobacco. Initially used as a narcotic, tobacco's popularity as a smoking substance would only rise in the years to follow.

The success of John Hawkins' first two slave voyages did not go unnoticed and stirred considerable ire among the Spanish authorities. This escalating tension led to Queen Elizabeth I taking a decisive step: she barred Hawkins from undertaking further seafaring expeditions. Undeterred and resourceful, Hawkins ingeniously circumvented this restriction by orchestrating another slave voyage, this time entrusting the command to a kinsman named John Lovell. Adding to the venture's notable lineage, Sir Francis Drake, who is believed to be a relative of Lovell, joined the expedition as well.

In 1566, under Lovell's leadership, the expedition set sail for the West African coast. Once there, Lovell, adopting a strategy of piracy reminiscent of Hawkins' own methods, captured five ships. Notably, three of these were already laden with enslaved individuals. Seizing both the human and material cargo, Lovell then navigated to the Spanish West Indies, intent on trading these ill-gotten gains.

However, the venture did not unfold as planned. The transaction of the cargo in the Spanish West Indies encountered significant difficulties. The situation deteriorated to such an extent that Lovell was forced to make a drastic decision. He abandoned 92 enslaved individuals ashore, leaving them without any payment or provision, a move born of desperation and indicative of the callous nature of the slave trade.

This ill-fated venture left an indelible mark on those involved. Sir Francis Drake, in later years, would reflect on the trip with a sense of embarrassment, a rare admission of regret in an era often defined by ruthless ambition and moral ambiguity. John Hawkins, for his part, attributed the failure of the venture not to the inherent risks or ethical quandaries of slave trading but to what he termed the "simpleness" of his deputies. This rationalization, casting blame on his subordinates rather than the perils and ethical implications of the slave trade itself.

Despite Queen Elizabeth I's previous prohibition against John Hawkins setting sail, her stance softened, and she eventually sanctioned his third slave voyage. Thus, on the 2nd of October 1567, Hawkins departed from Plymouth, setting his sights once again on the lucrative but ethically fraught business of slave trading. His journey to the African coast, however, was met with unforeseen challenges. Unlike his previous voyages, Hawkins found the local Portuguese agents decidedly resistant to trading with him, posing a significant obstacle to his usual means of acquiring enslaved individuals.

Undeterred, Hawkins resorted to more direct and violent methods. He launched an audacious attempt to capture the inhabitants of a village near Cape Verde. This reckless endeavor resulted in Hawkins sustaining an injury, forcing him to beat a hasty retreat. Not one to be easily dissuaded, Hawkins then sought the assistance of a local king in Sierra Leone. With this newfound alliance, he orchestrated the forcible kidnapping of over 500 people. By the

7th of February 1568, he was ready to cross the Atlantic Ocean, intent on selling these captives in the New World.

Hawkins' first stop was Margarita Province, where he managed to sell a portion of his human cargo. He then proceeded to Borburata, continuing his nefarious trade. However, in Rio de la Hacha, he encountered resistance from the local governor who refused him permission to trade. In response, Sir Francis Drake, accompanying Hawkins, took aggressive action by firing at the governor's house. This act of violence escalated into a full-blown battle, leading to Hawkins' forceful takeover of the town and the subsequent sale of the enslaved individuals.

The voyage took a dramatic turn at the Battle of San Juan de Ulúa, a fierce confrontation between English privateers, led by Hawkins, and Spanish forces. Hawkins' fleet, comprising six armed merchant ships, had been conducting trade alongside the Spanish, albeit through cooperation with local officials rather than official channels. The central Spanish authorities, viewing these activities as illegal smuggling, launched a sudden attack on Hawkins' fleet. In the chaos, Drake made a narrow escape aboard the Judith, while Hawkins suffered a crushing defeat. His surviving ship, the Minion, barely managed to limp home with a mere 15 crew members.

Despite the harrowing experiences and losses, the expedition was not without financial gain. Hawkins, demonstrating his shrewdness even in adversity, had managed to transfer most of his trading income onto the Minion. This strategic move ensured that, despite the moral and human costs, the voyage concluded with considerable economic profit.

In 1578, John Hawkins embarked on a new chapter in his illustrious career, being appointed as the Treasurer of the Navy. Initially, he worked in conjunction with his father-in-law, Benjamin Gonson, a seasoned naval administrator, but soon Hawkins assumed full control of the role. In this capacity, Hawkins displayed a remarkable flair for administration and reform, fundamentally transforming the Royal Navy's operations.

His tenure as Treasurer was marked by a series of significant reforms that reshaped the Navy both financially and structurally. One of his most notable achievements was the implementation of rigorous administrative reforms that led to substantial financial savings. Through careful management and strategic planning, Hawkins succeeded in saving nearly £4,000 annually—a considerable sum at the time. Simultaneously, he demonstrated a commitment to the welfare of the naval personnel by increasing their pay, an action that likely boosted morale and efficiency within the ranks.

Hawkins also turned his attention to the design of naval ships. With a visionary approach, he revolutionized the construction of galleons. Under his guidance, these ships were elongated, enabling them to carry more artillery. Furthermore, the design enhancements made the vessels more maneuverable and faster, significantly improving their performance in naval engagements. His innovations didn't stop at design; Hawkins also expanded the Navy's fleet. By 1587, under his stewardship, the Navy boasted 23 ships and 18 pinnaces, a testament to his dedication to strengthening England's maritime might.

The impact of Hawkins' reforms was profound. Historian Garrett Mattingly aptly summarized the result, stating that the Navy had become a "fighting-fleet faster and more weatherly than any that had ever been seen on the ocean before." This transformation was not just a matter of improved hardware; it represented a strategic advantage that would prove crucial in the naval conflicts of the era.

However, Hawkins' sweeping reforms and rising influence inevitably led to friction within the naval administration. His financial measures, in particular, disturbed individuals who had vested interests in the old systems. In 1582, this brewing discontent culminated in an accusation of administrative malfeasance by his rival, Sir William Wynter. This serious charge led to the establishment of a Royal Commission to investigate the allegations of fraud against Hawkins. The commission, comprising notable figures like William Cecil, 1st Baron Burghley, Francis Walsingham, and Sir Francis Drake, conducted a thorough review of Hawkins' tenure. In a resounding vindication of his integrity and competence, the commission concluded that there was no evidence of corruption. Furthermore, they affirmed that the Queen's Navy was in an exemplary condition, a clear endorsement of Hawkins' transformative leadership and the efficacy of his reforms.

John Hawkins, who rose to the esteemed rank of Vice-Admiral, played a pivotal role in the historic victory against the Spanish Armada. As a key member of the war council and third in command of the English fleet, his influence on the outcome of this monumental engagement was profound. Hawkins' contributions extended beyond his commanding presence; the enhanced ship designs he had pioneered during his tenure as Treasurer of the Navy proved to be game-changing. These innovations provided the English fleet with superior firepower and speed, crucial factors in their triumph over the Spanish Armada.

In the wake of this victory, Hawkins, ever the strategist, advocated for an aggressive approach against Spain. He proposed the seizure of King Philip II's colonial treasures, aiming to deplete Spain's financial resources and prevent the re-arming of its naval forces. In 1589, Hawkins joined forces with Francis Drake in what was known as the English Armada. A primary objective of this fleet was to intercept the treasure-laden Spanish ships returning from Mexico. Hawkins believed that a decisive victory here could potentially bring Philip II to the negotiating table, potentially shortening the conflict. However, this ambitious venture did not yield the desired results. The English Armada failed in its mission, allowing King Philip II a crucial opportunity to reinforce his naval capabilities. By the end of 1589, Spain had managed to reconstruct a formidable Atlantic fleet, once again capable of protecting its treasure ships on their journey home.

During this tumultuous period, Hawkins experienced a personal loss. In

1591, his wife Katherine Hawkins passed away. Subsequently, he remarried Margaret Vaughan, the daughter of Charles Vaughan and a Lady of the Bedchamber to Queen Elizabeth I.

The year 1593 brought further challenges for Hawkins. His son, Richard Hawkins, suffered defeat and was captured by the Spanish in a naval engagement known as the action of San Mateo Bay. Determined to rescue his son, Hawkins, in collaboration with his cousin Sir Francis Drake, organized a formidable fleet of 27 ships. Their mission was to launch an offensive against the Spanish in the West Indies. Departing from Plymouth on the 29th of August, 1595, the expedition faced numerous obstacles, including adverse weather conditions and skirmishes with the Spanish fleet. These challenges impeded their efforts to secure the release of Richard Hawkins.

Tragically, John Hawkins' life came to an end amidst this arduous campaign. On the 12th of November, 1595, it was reported that Hawkins had passed away at sea near Puerto Rico. His death marked the conclusion of a career that had significantly influenced the course of naval history, characterized by strategic brilliance, transformative naval reforms, and significant, albeit controversial, contributions to England's maritime dominance.

Guillaume Le Testu

uillaume Le Testu, also known as "Têtu," was a trailblazing navigator hailing from the bustling port of Le Havre in Normandy. Born into a distinguished family of ship captains and pilots who navigated the Atlantic and the Spanish Main from 1550-1640, Le Testu's heritage was as deep as the oceans he would come to explore.

The mysteries of his birth date, speculated to be between 1509-1512, add an aura of intrigue to his story. This estimate arises from a clue in his masterwork, the "Cosmographie Universelle" published in 1556, where he mentions his birth in the early 16th century. Le Testu's claim of being a native of Le Havre de Grace, a port that emerged around 1517, further shrouds his early years in mystery.

Le Testu's tale intertwines with the intriguing evolution of Le Havre, a place of historical debate. Was it a completely new town or an extension of the ancient Harfleur? The port, christened as Ville Françoise-de-Grâce in honor of King Francois I, grew around the sacred Notre-Dame-de-Grâce chapel, lending its name to the new harbor.

Le Testu's adventure truly began at Dieppe, where he honed his skills in navigation. By 1551, he set sail on the Salamandre for an epic voyage to Brazil, accompanied by André Thevet, a Franciscan friar and fellow cartographer. Their journey led them to chart territories as far as the Rio de la Plata, reaching the uncharted waters south of Rio de Janeiro and marking the beginnings of

São Francisco do Sul.

However, Le Testu's journey wasn't without peril. A fierce battle with Portuguese ships near Trinidad in late December left his ship, the Salamandre, heavily damaged. Despite this, his indomitable spirit and keen cartographic skills allowed him to map a significant portion of the South American coastline, culminating in his triumphant return to Dieppe in July 1552. Join us in uncovering the life and adventures of this remarkable figure, whose legacy is as vast as the seas he once navigated.

In the year 1555, a tale of high adventure unfurled as Guillaume Le Testu joined forces with Admiral Gaspard de Coligny and Nicolas Durand, known as Sieur de Villegagnon, on a daring colonizing expedition to Brazil. This quest wasn't just about expansion; it was a mission to create a safe haven for Huguenots, the French Protestants persecuted in Europe, in a land they envisioned as "France Antarctique."

Villegagnon, a man of noble lineage and a commander of the Knights of Malta, had grand ambitions. Beyond establishing a refuge for the Huguenots, he dreamed of tapping into Brazil's wealth of natural resources. The quest was driven by the lure of Brazilwood, a treasure sought after for its vibrant scarlet dye that enchanted the merchants of Rouen and its sturdy quality for construction. The very name of Brazil was derived from this coveted wood. Villegagnon's vision also included the exploration of rumored abundant precious metals and stones in this new land.

Evidence of their Brazilian endeavors can still be seen in the carved wood panels at the Museum of Antiquities in Rouen. These panels vividly depict the entire operation: from the logging and barking of Brazilwood, to its transportation and eventual loading onto ships anchored off the Brazilian coast.

The ambitious plan caught the attention of King Henry II of France, who endorsed it with a substantial funding of 10,000 livres. This financial boost was further supplemented by contributions from ship owners and merchants in Dieppe, including the renowned Jean d'Ango.

Faced with a shortage of volunteers, Villegagnon turned to the prisons of northern France, offering freedom to those willing to join this perilous journey. The result was a motley crew of 600, comprising French Huguenots, Swiss Calvinists seeking refuge from Catholic persecution, and a small personal guard of eight Scots for Villegagnon himself. The expedition also included an indigenous Tabajara native, a master of the Tupi language, to act as an interpreter. To keep their true destination a secret from the Portuguese ambassador in France, Villegagnon cleverly spread rumors of a voyage to the coast of Guinea.

Their journey was marked by challenges from the start. Departing from Le Havre De Grace on 12 July, 1555, the fleet was forced to return twice to the port of Dieppe due to harsh weather conditions. It wasn't until August 14 that they finally embarked on their grand voyage to South America. After three months at sea, on November 10th, the fleet discreetly anchored in the Bay of Guanabara, strategically avoiding the Tupi-occupied coast.

André Thévet, a cosmographer and contemporary of Guillaume Le Testu, chronicled their intrepid voyages between 1555 and 1556. Thévet's master-piece, "Les singularitez de la France antarctique," published in 1557, stands as a pioneering work in American ethnography. This narrative transcends mere travel documentation; it's a panoramic exploration of the French settlement and the indigenous Tupi tribes along the Brazilian coast, as seen through the eyes of a cosmographer - a geographer with a bird's-eye view of his subject.

Thévet's account is a treasure trove of first-hand observations, unveiling the intricate tapestry of Tupi life. He delves into their unique makeup practices, dietary habits, and warfare techniques, painting a vivid picture of a culture rich in tradition and complexity. His narrative goes further, shedding light on their spiritual beliefs, myths, and customs. The details extend to the natural world, providing accurate descriptions of the local wildlife and plants vital to the Tupi, including wild boar, deer, sweet potatoes, tobacco, cassava, cashews, and pineapples. Claude Lévi-Strauss, the esteemed French anthropologist, hailed Thévet's work as a crucial source of knowledge about the now-lost tribes of South America's coast.

The Tupi, formidable warriors with no unified identity or nation, were constantly engaged in conflicts with neighboring tribes or within their own ranks. Their wars were not mere battles for dominance but ritualistic endeavors, where capturing enemies for cannibalistic rites was common. This practice was believed to imbue them with the strength of their foes.

For the French settlers, the Portuguese presented a significant challenge. Having colonized the Brazilian coasts since the early 16th century, the Portuguese were already well-established. However, their conflicts with the principal Tupi tribes turned into an unintended advantage for the French. Despite initial apprehensions about the Tupi's cannibalistic rituals, the French found unlikely allies in them against their common Portuguese enemy.

The French set their sights on an island for their colony, known to the Tupi as Serigipe and called "French Island" by the settlers. Today, it is recognized as Villegagnon Island. Although rocky and sparse, the island provided a strategic defensive position against both sea and land attacks. Here, the French swiftly erected houses, unloaded men, weapons, ammunition, and tools, and adapted to the native hunting methods and local fauna.

In his "Les singularitez de la France antarctique," Thévet refers to these early settlers as Canadie or Canadiens, providing some of the earliest sketches and images of French Canadian settlers in the Americas.

The early French Huguenot settlers, known as "Canadiens," quickly adapted to their new surroundings by learning from the Tupi. They mastered the art of spearing wild boar and other game, and then smoking the meat on a wooden platform, a technique resting on sticks over a sacred fire. This method gave rise to the French word "boucan," stemming from the Tupi term for a rack used for roasting or storing things. The term "buccaneer" also has its roots in this practice, derived from the Arawak word "buccan," a wooden frame for smoking meat. The hunters who employed these frames became known as "boucaniers," and the practice became so widespread in the New World that French Huguenots in the Caribbean were collectively dubbed Buccaneers.

André Thévet, a meticulous chronicler, is credited with documenting the use of the tobacco plant, known as "Petun" by the Tupi. This term eventually became the original French word for tobacco. When Thévet returned to France in 1557, he brought with him a strain of tobacco for cultivation at his home in Angouleme. Interestingly, while Thévet was the first to cultivate tobacco in Europe, it is Jean Nicot, the French ambassador to Lisbon, who is often credited for introducing tobacco to the European continent. Nicot brought back a different strain in 1559 for Catherine de' Medici and the French court, leading to the plant's designation as "Nicotiana."

Notably, the strain Thévet brought from Brazil was "Nicotiana tobacum," the variety almost universally used today. In contrast, Nicot's "Nicotiana rustica" strain, originally from Florida, is primarily grown in Turkey now.

Despite numerous challenges, the European settlers, with the assistance of the Tupi, constructed Fort Coligny in just three months. Initially, the fort featured five batteries pointing towards the sea. However, as time progressed, the Tupi workforce grew disillusioned with their rewards from the French and became increasingly aware of the disproportionate workload, with the French shirking the heavier tasks. Signs of discontent began to emerge among the indigenous helpers. Meanwhile, the colonists themselves also grappled with the harsh realities and difficulties of life on the island, leading to growing dissatisfaction within the settlement.

Faced with growing challenges, Villegagnon implemented strict measures to maintain control over the French settlement. He curtailed extended trips to the mainland, primarily to limit the interactions between the French settlers and the native population. Although he sought strong ties with the Tupi tribes, Villegagnon observed that sailors and colonists were increasingly adopting native rites and traditions, often forsaking their own religious practices. In an attempt to regulate personal relationships, he mandated that any French sailors or colonists involved with native women marry them under French law and reside on the island.

However, these stringent rules led to mounting discontent within the colony. Many settlers, disillusioned with the regime, seized opportunities provided by passing commercial vessels to escape back to France. The cultural clash over issues like cannibalism, practiced by the Tupi allies, further exacerbated tensions. Villegagnon's harsh discipline, coupled with these internal conflicts, threatened the fragile balance of the French establishment in the New World.

Within just three months of the colony's founding, Villegagnon penned a report detailing the situation and requesting reinforcements and supplies from the King. He entrusted this report to Le Testu for delivery to Le Havre.

A dramatic turn of events unfolded on February 14, 1556, just two days after Le Testu and Andrew Thevet departed for France. A conspiracy, led by a French settler forced into marriage with a Tupi woman, aimed to assassinate Villegagnon, who was guarded by only eight Scottish soldiers. The conspirators planned to recruit a disgruntled guard by bribing him, but their scheme unraveled when the guard, only pretending to cooperate, exposed their plot to Nicolas Barré, a former pilot and Villegagnon's aide.

The fallout from this failed coup was severe. The ringleader escaped, but two conspirators were tried, convicted, and hanged by the colony's council, while others faced lighter sentences. This harsh crackdown led to further discord. Many settlers chose to abandon the colony, living in the woods with the indigenous people, some being forced into marriages, and others rebelling and facing the death penalty.

In time, the colony splintered. A faction of the Huguenots, disillusioned by what they perceived as Villegagnon's tyrannical rule, chose exile over subjugation. They ventured onto the mainland, seeking a more favorable location than enduring the harsh conditions under the self-styled "King of America." This group established a new settlement, Henryville, on the mainland, directly facing the island, marking yet another chapter in the tumultuous history of "France Antarctique."

In April 1556, Guillaume Le Testu returned to Le Havre bearing the critical report from the New World. During this period, the religious strife between Catholics and Protestants in France had escalated, with Admiral Gaspard de Coligny embracing Protestantism. Villegagnon, who had aligned himself with Calvinist doctrines, envisioned the Brazilian colony as a sanctuary for French Protestants. Alongside Le Testu and Thevet, he sent a letter requesting Calvinist pastors for the colony and proposed the relocation of thousands of persecuted Protestants from France to Brazil.

Responding to this call, a new expedition was organized, including two pastors: Pierre Richer, a man in his fifties, and Guillaume Chartier, a young theology student from Geneva. The group also included a shoemaker and theologian, Jean de Lery, who would later document his experiences, and nine others, including Guillaume Le Testu. Funded by Coligny and Villegagnon, the expedition, comprising three hundred settlers and five young women destined to marry in Brazil, departed from Le Havre on November 19, 1556.

Their voyage, however, faced immediate challenges. Unable to resupply with food or fresh water in the Canary Islands, which were under Spanish control, the expedition resorted to piracy and privateering, raiding Spanish and Portuguese vessels to gather the necessary provisions. The scarcity of resources led to strict rationing of water and food, minimizing the need for confrontations with enemy ships. Despite these adversities, the expedition maintained strict discipline, crucial for the success of their journey.

It was amidst these turbulent voyages that Le Testu likely began penning his "Cosmographie Universelle," a work that would later cement his legacy. This manuscript, started on the high seas, under challenging conditions, would go on to be a significant contribution to the understanding of the geography and cultures of the New World.

The "Cosmographie Universelle," a remarkable atlas by Guillaume Le Testu, stands as a tribute to his mentor and patron, Admiral Gaspard de Coligny, a prominent Huguenot leader. This comprehensive work, composed of 56 maps, was crafted from an array of charts sourced from French, Spanish, and Portuguese origins, provided by Coligny and meticulously drawn by Le Testu. His outstanding efforts earned him royal recognition, leading to his appointment as an official Royal Pilot by King Henry II.

One intriguing feature of Le Testu's atlas is its depiction of a southern continent, uncharted at the time, accompanied by the assertion: "not imaginary even though no one has found it." This atlas is also noteworthy for its accurate portrayals of the Baja Peninsula, the Pacific Ocean, Canada, and even Alaska.

The expedition, carrying the hopes of bolstering the French presence in the New World, arrived at Villegagnon Island in Guanabara Bay on March 7, 1557. Despite his initial disappointment with the reinforcement's composition, Villegagnon welcomed the newcomers warmly. However, in a correspondence to John Calvin dated March 31, 1557, he candidly expressed his concerns and challenges.

By early 1558, after the Calvinist ministers had returned to France, Ville-gagnon found himself leading a diminished force of just 80 men, comprised of Scots and French. Facing accusations over his leadership, he returned to

France in 1559 to defend himself, leaving his nephew, Bois-le-Comte, in charge of the colony.

Upon his return to France by the end of 1559, Villegagnon was disillusioned by the internal religious strife within the small colony, particularly troubled by Calvinist doctrines on the Eucharist. His departure aimed at securing additional support and resources for the colony, but the intensifying conflict with the Calvinists diverted the Crown's focus from colonial ventures. Following the colony's fall to the Portuguese, Villegagnon relinquished his claims to France Antarctique in exchange for 30,000 écus from the Portuguese Crown.

Villegagnon's later years saw a reversal in his stance on Calvinism. He actively opposed the Protestants, participating in the suppression of the Amboise conspiracy. From 1568, he represented the Order of Malta at the French Court and became the Commander of the Order's Commandery in Beauvais. In 1569, he published "De Consecratione, mystico sacrificio et duplici Christi oblatione," a controversial work on the Eucharist, before passing away on January 9, 1571.

After the dissolution of the French Colony in Brazil, Le Testu returned to France at the end of 1559. It's speculated that he might have ventured to Africa and North America, participating in the burgeoning triangular trade between Africa, the New World colonies, and Europe. Additionally, there are suggestions that he scouted northern locations for a new French Huguenot colony.

Leveraging his extensive travels and the insights gleaned from fellow explorers, Guillaume Le Testu meticulously revised his world map in 1566, significantly enhancing the depiction of the mythical southern continent compared to his initial 1556 portolan. This updated map, titled "Mappemonde en deux hémisphères," aimed to accurately represent the latitude and longitude of the world. His maps are notably among the first to detail the coast of Canada and its surroundings.

Le Testu's adventures also took him to the Isle of Tortuga in the Caribbean, well before its notoriety as a pirate haven. His knowledge of this region was enriched by interactions with other pilots and captains. Although frequented by French Corsairs like Le Testu before 1600, Tortuga had not yet become the infamous pirate hub of later years:

"Seuls les épigones d'Ango (Guillaume Le Testu, Leclerc Jambe-de-Bois, Jean Bontemps, Menjouyn de La Cabane, etc.) continuent à opérer dans le golfe du Mexique et la mer des Antilles, en particulier à partir de l'île de la Tortue."

This translates roughly to: "Only the captains of Jean D'Ango's fleet (Guillaume Testu, Leclerc Leg-of-Wood, Jean Bontemps, Menjouyn of the Hut, etc.) continue to operate in the Gulf of Mexico and the Caribbean Sea, particularly from the island of Tortuga."

During the 1500s, France was deeply embroiled in religious turmoil. The nation, long Catholic, saw the introduction of Lutheranism in the 1520s. By 1534, Lutheranism posed a significant threat to Catholic dominance, prompting the crown to take aggressive measures to suppress it. John Calvin, a Frenchman himself and a vocal proponent of Protestant ideals, espoused Calvinism, garnering substantial support by the 1540s. The 1550s witnessed many noblemen siding with the Protestants, challenging the established church and leading to a division of France into two major religious factions: the Catholics and the Calvinists, now known as Huguenots. This escalating tension erupted into violence in the spring of 1562.

The conflict was briefly paused in 1563 with the Edict of Amboise, which granted limited worship rights to the Huguenots. However, this was a strategic move by the crown as they sought to consolidate support against a potential alliance with Spain. The truce was short-lived, and warfare resumed in 1567, fueled by fears of a Spanish alliance. It was during this period of renewed conflict that Le Testu actively engaged in raids on behalf of the Huguenot cause. His raiding campaign lasted through 1567 and 1568 until he was ultimately captured by the Catholics.

Filippo Strozzi, a notable figure in the French court, petitioned Catherine de Medici, the Queen of France, for the release of Guillaume Le Testu from Spanish captivity. His efforts bore fruit when, in June 1571, Charles IX of France wrote to his cousin, King Philip II of Spain, requesting Le Testu's release. After nearly four years of imprisonment, a report from the secretary confirmed Le Testu's freedom on January 30, 1572. Strozzi's interest in Le Testu was not solely compassionate; he recognized Le Testu's exceptional skills as a navigator, likely influenced by his maps depicting "imaginary continents" presented to the King.

Equipped by Strozzi, Le Testu became the captain of an 80-ton warship, "Le Havre," commanding a crew of about 70 men. Le Testu's prominence in privateering and piracy history is notably marked by his encounter with Sir Francis Drake in February 1573 off the coast of Panama. Le Testu, in dire need of fresh water due to dysentery afflicting his crew, approached Drake. Drake responded generously, sending drink, fresh meat, and an invitation to follow him to the next port for further supplies.

Upon anchoring, Le Testu sent Drake a case of pistols and a gilt scimitar, a token of appreciation from Coligny, previously owned by Filippo Strozzi and bestowed upon Le Testu by Henry II for his atlas. Drake reciprocated with a gold chain and an enamel tablet.

The meeting between these two captains was marked by mutual respect and shared experiences. Le Testu revealed to Drake his Huguenot background and his presence in France during the St. Bartholomew's Day Massacre. Seeking refuge from persecution, he turned to the sea, operating as a French Privateer off the Spanish Main. Le Testu, aware of Drake's successes against the Spanish, sought an alliance, offering his ship, crew, and navigational expertise.

Drake, recognizing the value of Le Testu's experience, agreed to a partnership. The two formed a "provisional Entente Cordiale," uniting against their common enemy, Spain.

Le Testu's presence near Panama has sparked scholarly debate. Spanish records from that era suggested a planned French expedition in 1572. While many historians believe Le Testu was independently seeking fortune, like Drake, backed by Venetian financiers, it's plausible that his primary aim was exploration. This objective, potentially to precede the Spanish in discovering Australia and the northern Pacific coast, would align with France's broader exploratory ambitions. The wealth accrued from the Caribbean and the southern Pacific could finance a more extensive expedition to Australia and perhaps the Pacific Northwest, a journey eventually completed nearly two centuries later by English Captain James Cook.

While the English crew shared common goals with Guillaume Le Testu, there remained a degree of mistrust towards the French, with a preference for the local Cimaroons as allies. Ultimately, it was Testu's skill as a pilot, the size of his ship, and the strength of his crew that proved pivotal in securing their cooperation.

Testu, a seasoned navigator, was highly regarded by the much younger Drake, who valued his advice and insight. Testu theorized that a passage south of the Straits of Magellan could offer an easier route around the tip of South America. His charts later guided Drake to discover this passage, which became known as Drake's Passage, serving as the primary route for circumnavigating South America until the Panama Canal's opening.

Following an agreement on their collaborative venture, the united forces of French, English, and Cimaroons set sail for Rio Francisco on Brazil's coast. Their mission was to intercept a mule train laden with gold and silver en route from Panama to Nombre de Dios. After positioning themselves about a mile from the main route, they spent a night nearby, overhearing carpenters working on ships in Nombre de Dios.

Their plan came to fruition on April 1st when a mule train approached, and they launched a successful attack. Le Testu's share of the spoils was substantial, estimated at around £20,000. However, during the engagement, he sustained a serious stomach wound from hail shot. Opting not to continue with Drake, Le Testu decided to rest in the woods until he was fit to travel, leaving two of his men with him. The rest of the party moved on to their scheduled fleet rendezvous.

As they neared the rendezvous point, instead of finding their English pinnaces, they were confronted by a Spanish fleet. Drake was compelled to construct a raft and sail to an island about three leagues offshore to contact his ships.

Once safely reunited with his crew, Drake swiftly planned a rescue mission for Captain Testu and to recover the remaining buried silver. However, his men, concerned for his safety, insisted that he not participate directly in this perilous endeavor. Leadership of the mission was thus assigned to John Oxenham and Thomas Sherwell, with Drake accompanying them only as far as the Francisco River, where he assisted with rowing one of the pinnaces.

As they navigated the river, a dramatic scene unfolded. One of Captain Testu's companions, who had been left to guard the injured captain, emerged from the reeds, collapsing to his knees in relief and gratitude at the sight of Drake's men. He recounted a harrowing tale of their encounter with the Spaniards, which had occurred just half an hour after he had begun his watch by Testu's side. As the Spaniards approached, he and his mate fled, discarding their loot in the haste of escape. His comrade, slowed down by the weight of a box of jewels he had retrieved, was soon captured by the Spaniards, along with Captain Testu.

Tragically, the French privateer Captain Testu was reportedly executed by the Spaniards, his head displayed prominently in the marketplace of Nombre de

Dios as a grim warning.

The intelligence and navigational insights provided by Testu, however, were not in vain. Drake later successfully navigated the passage between the southernmost point of the American continent and Antarctica. This accomplishment laid the groundwork for his subsequent renowned expedition along the Pacific Coast, reaching as far north as the Arctic. This remarkable journey and Drake's exploits were later immortalized in William Davenant's opera "The History Of Sir Francis Drake," first performed in 1659, celebrating the enduring legacy of these adventurous seafarers.

Grace O'Malley

Grace O'Malley, often maligned by her English foes as "a woman who hath imprudently passed the part of womanhood," stands as a complex figure in history. Overlooked by her contemporaries in Irish chronicling, her story, nonetheless, wove itself into the rich tapestry of native folklore. As time progressed, Irish nationalists elevated her to a legendary status, hailing her as Gráinne Mhaol, an emblematic warrior. In their narratives, she would heroically lead Irish soldiers across the sea to vanquish the English, embodying the spirit of resistance and national pride.

Her legend continued to evolve, cementing her place as an icon in the arena of international feminism. Grace O'Malley was celebrated not only as a paragon of strength and independence but also as a symbol of the struggles against the misogynistic laws of her time. Her life and legacy have inspired a plethora of artistic and cultural works, ranging from poetry and music to romantic novels, documentaries, and even an interpretive center dedicated to her life.

Yet, the mystique surrounding Gráinne Ní Máille is akin to a double-edged sword. While it has ensured the endurance of her name through the ages, it has also cast a veil over the actuality of her existence. The legend often overshadows the woman, obscuring the true facets of her life. She was, undeniably, an extraordinary figure – a woman who navigated, fought, and persevered through a tumultuous era in Irish history. This was a time marked by the disintegration of the Gaelic order and the devastation of Ireland's ruling elite, a period that shaped the very fabric of Irish identity.

To truly understand the person behind the myth of Grace O'Malley, it's essential to delve into the historical context of her era, the adversities she faced, and the societal structure that shaped her. The early 16th century in Ireland was a time of stark cultural dichotomy. On one side, Dublin, its adjacent counties, and various coastal cities fell under English rule. These regions viewed their hinterlands with a mix of fear and apprehension, embodying a frontier-like mentality. In contrast, the rest of Ireland was a mosaic of Gaelicised Old English and native Irish communities. These groups lived in self-governing territories, engaging in traditional activities like cattle raiding, castle seizing, feuding, intermarrying, and vying for supremacy.

This society was underpinned by a system of clientship, where lesser families allied themselves with more powerful ones. These alliances were solidified through tribute, military aid, marriages, and fostering relationships. The Uí Máilles, to whom Grace belonged, were clients of the Mayo Bourkes (MacWilliam Iachtarach) and had their own sub-clients. This network operated under strict laws, creating a complex interdependence and a hierarchical society where status and honor were highly valued.

The reign of Henry VIII marked a pivotal shift in Ireland's history. Proclaiming himself "King of Ireland," Henry VIII set in motion a new Crown policy. No longer content with merely holding their Irish territories, English monarchs sought to halt the Gaelicisation of the Old English and to Anglicise the entire population. This led to policies like 'Surrender and Regrant,' which appealed to many of Ireland's ruling elite, reshaping the traditional power structures.

During Queen Elizabeth's reign, significant changes swept through Gaelic Ireland. Settlements and plantations by English adventurers, who often doubled as Crown officials, began to spread. These developments, along with Elizabeth's commitment to the Reformation and the displacement of the old ruling classes by newcomers, inevitably sparked violence and social unrest.

Gráinne O'Malley emerged from this tumultuous backdrop. Born around 1530 to Owen Dubhdara Uí Máille and Margaret Ní Máille, she was an heir to the Gaelic aristocracy. The O'Malleys, along with their neighbors, the O'Flahertys, were unique among Gaelic families in their dual reliance on land and sea for livelihood. Dubhdara Uí Máille engaged in diverse activities, from trading raw materials for luxury goods to ferrying Scottish mercenaries, fishing, opportunistic piracy, and enforcing tolls on shipping within their waters. The O'Malleys thrived as an independent clan, navigating a complex network of tribute and allegiance.

Gráinne O'Malley's early life is shrouded in mystery, as details about the upbringing of Gaelic nobility, particularly women, during the 16th century are scarce. However, existing historical sources suggest that noblewomen of that era in Ireland received a relatively good education. In 1546, Gráinne married Dónal-an-Chogaidh O'Flaherty, the tánaiste or heir presumptive of the O'Flaherty clan. This union produced two sons and a daughter. As a chieftain's daughter, Gráinne likely brought a significant dowry, or spréidh, to the marriage. Under Gaelic law, while the dowry could be utilized by the husband, it was required to be returned in full to the wife if the marriage ended. This process often involved strict sureties, and wives sometimes had to resort to legal means to reclaim their dowry.

In these marriages, women maintained control over their personal properties, which they brought into the union. They were also entitled to independently acquire additional assets, which could range from troops and ships to various other goods. Gráinne's actions during her marriage suggest that her personal property might have included galleys and men. This is further supported by the fact that she owned at least three galleys after Dónal-an-Chogaidh's death.

Popular lore often portrays Gráinne as assuming leadership roles due to Dónal-an-Chogaidh's perceived incompetence. He was known for his quick temper and impulsive nature, frequently engaging in feuds, notably with the

Joyces. In 1564, another significant figure, Murrough-na-dTuadh O'Flaherty, endeavored to expand his territory. This move caught the attention of the Crown authorities, who saw an opportunity to employ their 'divide and conquer' strategy. They struck a deal with Murrough-na-dTuadh, granting him overlordship of Iar Chonnacht and thus jeopardizing Dónal-na-Chogaidh's position as tánaiste.

Before Dónal could respond to these developments, he suffered a fatal injury during a clash with the Joyces. Tradition credits Gráinne with seeking vengeance for her husband's death. She is famed for leading, or according to some accounts, repelling an attack on the strategically important Cock's Castle in Lough Corrib. Her bravery in this encounter was so noteworthy that the castle was subsequently known as Hen's Castle, a testament to her courage and leadership.

Under the Gaelic legal system, Gráinne O'Malley couldn't inherit O'Flaherty lands, leading her to return to Umhall and establish herself on Clare Island. This move is often interpreted as a forced exile due to misogynistic legal constraints, despite her proven leadership skills. However, it's crucial to note that Gaelic law empowered women with complete control over their own property. This contrasts sharply with English common law of the time, where a woman's property automatically transferred to her husband upon marriage, and she was only entitled to a life interest in a portion of the property, typically one-third, after his death.

Once settled on Clare Island, Gráinne vigorously pursued her livelihood through maritime activities, commanding three galleys and several smaller boats. This period marked the inception of her legacy as the 'pirate queen' of Connacht. Piracy, a common and relatively unsophisticated practice in Ireland, involved coastal raids, imposing tolls on passing ships, and plundering unprotected vessels.

In her 1593 petition to Queen Elizabeth, Gráinne rationalized her actions, citing the turbulent times where

'discord . . . and dissention . . . [where] every chieftain . . . took arms by strong hand to make head against his neighbours which in like manner constrained your highness fond subject to take arms and by force to maintain herself and her people'.

Assessing the extent of Gráinne's activities during this period is challenging. She is often credited with raids spanning from Donegal to Waterford. One notable story involves her response to being denied hospitality by the Earl of Howth. According to the tale, Gráinne kidnapped his heir, demanding as ransom a permanent extra place set at each meal at Howth Castle. While later historians attribute this story to Richard-na-Iarainn Bourke, records at Howth Castle acknowledge Gráinne's involvement.

The size and composition of Gráinne's fleet remain largely speculative. Estimates range from five to twenty ships, varying in size. These vessels, primarily small, agile, and equipped for both oar and sail, were ideal for coastal navigation but not suited for open sea voyages.

When Gráinne O'Malley married Richard-na-Iarainn Bourke of Burrishoole and Carra in 1567, she maintained control over her fleet and continued her maritime ventures. Richard-na-Iarainn's territory spanned the northern shores of Clew Bay, with his primary residence at Carraigahowley Castle. A popular but unverified legend suggests that their marriage was initially intended to be provisional, lasting only one year. This narrative goes on to describe how, at the end of this period, Richard-na-Iarainn supposedly found himself locked out of Carraigahowley by Gráinne, in what has been romantically interpreted as their divorce.

However, this story lacks substantiation from Gaelic legal traditions, and their later life together paints a different picture. Gráinne and Richard-na-Iarainn continued to live and function as a married couple until his death. Contrary to the implications of the legend, Gráinne stayed at Carraigahowley instead of returning to Umhall, which would have been customary had their marriage legally ended. Upon Richard's knighthood, Gráinne adopted the title Lady Bourke and accompanied him to formal events. This ongoing partnership suggests that the supposed eviction may have been a temporary outcome of a dispute, considering the strong-willed natures of both Gráinne and Richard.

The birth of their child, Tibbot-na-Long, is enveloped in its own layer of mythology. He was allegedly born aboard one of Gráinne's galleys. In a dramatic turn of events, it's said that just a day after giving birth, Gráinne was thrust into a confrontation with Algerian corsairs attacking their ship. According to this tale, she emerged from her childbirth bed and played a crucial role in repelling the attackers, showcasing her remarkable resilience and leadership even in the most challenging circumstances.

The year 1569 marked a turning point in Connacht's history with the appointment of Sir Edward Fitton as the provincial president, signaling the Crown's intensified efforts to subdue the region. After the Battle of Shrule in 1570, the MacWilliam clan agreed to pay an annual rent of 200 marks to the Crown, though the clan leader died soon after. Shane MacOliverus Bourke was then elected as the new MacWilliam, with Richard-na-Iarainn Bourke, Gráinne O'Malley's husband, as his tánaiste (heir presumptive).

In 1575, during his third term, Lord Deputy Sir Henry Sidney visited Connacht to implement a new taxation system known as 'composition.' Despite initial challenges, Sidney returned in 1576 and convened a meeting with the regional lords. It was during this visit that he encountered Gráinne O'Malley, whom he described as 'a most feminine sea captain called Granny Imallye' who offered her services and fleet to him. Sidney declined her offer of 'three galleys and two hundred fighting men', but he did take her assistance to inspect Galway's coastal defenses, a service for which she charged him. Sidney acknowledged Gráinne's influence and power, noting her as 'a notorious woman in all the coasts of Ireland.'

Shortly after her encounter with Sidney, Gráinne embarked on a raid in Desmond but was captured and imprisoned in Limerick Gaol, intended as a bargaining tool in the political chess game of the time. During her imprisonment, Lord Grey de Wilton succeeded Sidney. The political landscape shifted, and Richard-na-Iarainn's position as the next MacWilliam was thrown into uncertainty. In 1578, Desmond, seeking to demonstrate his loyalty to the Crown, handed Gráinne over to Lord Justice Drury. This act was well-received by Elizabeth's privy council.

Gráinne was released in 1579 and returned to Carraigahowley, where she soon faced a siege led by Captain Martin, who was tasked with capturing her for alleged attacks on Galway's shipping. Martin narrowly avoided being captured himself, as Gráinne and her defenders robustly repelled the assault, further cementing her reputation as an extraordinary and formidable figure.

In July 1579, James FitzMaurice Fitzgerald initiated an insurrection in Munster, aiming to start a 'holy war'. The newly appointed provincial president of Connacht, Sir Nicholas Malby, was tasked to suppress this uprising. By November, the earl of Desmond was branded a traitor, and his plea for aid to the MacWilliam was rejected. Richard-na-Iarainn, seizing the opportunity, raided the territories of O'Kelly and Lord Athenry.

In February 1580, Malby, briefly back in Connacht, quickly responded to Richard-na-Iarainn's actions by fortifying Burrishoole. The region's power dynamics became more complicated with Shane MacOliverus's death, as his brother claimed his titles and lands. Richard-na-Iarainn, joining forces with Gráinne, mobilized nearly 2000 troops. Facing rebellious activity in Munster, Malby and de Wilton were forced to comply with the duo's demands. Consequently, on April 16, 1580, Richard-na-Iarainn was granted nobility and the title of MacWilliam, agreeing to abide by English laws, pay rent to the Crown, and provide sustenance for 200 soldiers annually for 42 days.

By 1582, Lord and Lady Bourke had relocated to Lough Mask Castle. In May,

Richard-na-Iarainn, under the guise of collecting overdue rent, invaded Richard MacOliverus's domain with Malby's forces. In a twist of fate, the next year, Malby's representative, Theobald Dillon, while trying to collect rent, was threatened by Richard-na-Iarainn and Gráinne, the latter declaring her readiness to engage in combat.

Richard-na-Iarainn passed away of natural causes in April 1583. Gráinne, asserting her rights, gathered her followers, cattle, and horses, and moved to Carraigahowley, also taking her fleet. At 53, Gráinne Ní Máille was a prosperous, autonomous woman, adeptly navigating both English and local legal systems. However, her challenges were far from over.

In 1584, Sir John Perrot was appointed lord deputy, while Sir Richard Bingham became the provincial president of Connacht. Perrot's mission was to mitigate the estrangement caused by the severe tactics of his forerunners, favoring a reconciliatory approach. However, Bingham believed that force, not diplomacy, was the key to subduing the Irish. In 1585, Perrot introduced a new composition, promoting Surrender and Regrant and aiming to end clientship tributes. Meanwhile, Bingham, preferring aggressive methods, fixated on Gráinne as a troublemaker. He captured her son Tibbot-na-Long and detained him in Ballymote Castle for a year.

Bingham's task was to enforce the new composition in Connacht. During its first implementation in Mayo in 1585, some Bourkes, barricaded in Hag's Castle at Lough Mask, refused to comply. Bingham attacked and destroyed the castle. After the death of the MacWilliam, Bingham favored MacOliverus's eldest son for the title, overlooking Edmund Bourke of Castlebar. This led to a Bourke uprising, joined by the Uí Máilles and Richard 'the Devil's Hook' Bourke, Gráinne's son-in-law. Bingham then ordered his brother John to confiscate the lands of Gráinne's son Owen, who was allegedly murdered under controversial circumstances.

Outraged by her son's death, Gráinne actively opposed Bingham, who attempted to capture her. Released on the Devil's Hook's pledge, she soon fled to Ulster, either for aid or due to fear. Her exile lasted three months due to storm damage to her fleet.

By late 1587, the Bourke rebellion had dissipated, and Bingham was dispatched to Flanders. Gráinne seized this opportunity to appeal to Sir John Perrot in Dublin, securing a pardon for herself and her children. Amidst the 1588 Spanish Armada crisis, Bingham was recalled, replaced by Sir William Fitzwilliam, and instructed to eliminate any Spanish survivors, particularly in the Devil's Hook's region.

The final Bourke rebellion erupted in 1589 when Bingham commanded troops to attack the rebels. Gráinne ravaged the Aran Isles, contributing to widespread chaos in Connacht. Queen Elizabeth instructed Fitzwilliam to pacify the Bourkes, who, alongside English officials, accused Bingham of misconduct. Although acquitted in 1590, Bingham's return intensified the conflict, particularly against Gráinne, whose lands and fleet he decimated. Her son, Murrough-na-Moar, who sided with Bingham, faced her wrath.

In 1592, Tibbot-na-Long led a revolt against Bingham, while Gráinne suffered further losses as Bingham seized her property and fleet, leaving her destitute. Eventually, Tibbot-na-Long surrendered.

Gráinne, left with nothing, directly appealed to Queen Elizabeth I. In a 1593 petition, she highlighted her age and impoverishment, vowing to fight against the Queen's enemies in exchange for a modest livelihood and the restoration of her confiscated property. Around the same time, the Earl of Tyrone was covertly orchestrating a rebellion against the Crown, implicating Tibbot-na-Long who was then imprisoned on treason charges.

Concerned about Tibbot's fate and potentially facing execution without a fair trial, Gráinne took a bold step by sailing to London to make a personal appeal. From June to September, she was at the royal court, responding to Lord

Treasurer Burghley's inquiries. She narrated her compelled seafaring life, the aftermath of her son Owen's murder, and her subsequent mistreatment by Richard Bingham, including her confiscation of property and capture by John Bingham. She claimed to have lived as a farmer since receiving Perrot's pardon.

Bingham, infuriated by Gráinne's actions, wrote to the court claiming he had enough evidence to execute her. Despite his protests, Elizabeth agreed to hear Gráinne's plea and ordered an investigation. The only substantial charge against Gráinne was her punishment of her son Murrough-na-Moar; her other actions were overlooked as temporary deviations from the norm. Elizabeth sanctioned Tibbot-na-Long's release and arranged for a pension for Gráinne, funded by taxes from her sons' estates, instructing Bingham to ensure their peaceful and secure livelihood. She trusted Gráinne would remain a loyal subject.

Bingham, however, was hesitant to adhere to the Queen's directives. Aware that Gráinne was permitted to return to sea without restrictions, he assigned troops to monitor her and stationed a detachment on her lands, forcing her to provide for them. Facing near poverty, Gráinne once again sought Elizabeth's intervention in 1595, desiring security for her life. A commission was established to examine her claims, while Bingham, facing new accusations, fled to England and was detained.

In December 1595, during Tyrone's uprising, Red Hugh O'Donnell appointed his choice as MacWilliam, took hostages, and repeatedly raided Mayo, directing attacks on Gráinne. She persisted in rebuilding through familiar means. The Bourkes, including Gráinne, had to choose between supporting Elizabeth or O'Donnell. In 1597, Tibbot-na-Long secured favorable terms with the Crown. Bingham's successor, Sir Conyers Clifford, recorded a payment to Tibbot, Gráinne, and her other son for their services.

The final recorded incident involving Gráinne was in 1601, when an English warship captain reported an encounter with her galley, crewed with formidable forces. Gráinne Ní Máille is believed to have passed away in 1603.

Gráinne Ní Máille's legacy extends beyond the myths of a pirate queen or an Irish icon. She was a resilient, astute woman who consistently fought for her family's rights, rebuilding fortunes through land and sea ventures. Her adversaries were those who threatened her family's well-being, regardless of their ethnicity. Gráinne utilized every available means, including manipulating truths, much like her adversaries bent the law. She skillfully navigated the misunderstandings of English officials, seizing opportunities as they arose. Ultimately, she endured as a survivor, preserving her family's status even when other nobles were exiled.

Francis Drake

Francis Drake's early life is shrouded in a blend of mystery and historical intrigue, beginning with his birth at the pastoral Crowndale Farm, nestled in the picturesque landscape of Tavistock, Devon, England. The exact date of his birth remains a subject of scholarly debate, as formal records from that era are sparse. Some historians, like E. F. Benson, speculate that Drake's birth occurred during the turbulent times when the Six Articles of 1539 were in effect. However, this claim is contested by naval historian Julian Corbett, who critically examines William Camden's accounts, suggesting a possible memory lapse regarding Edmund Drake's (Francis' father) persecution under the Six Articles Act of 1539.

Efforts to pinpoint Drake's birth year rely on interpreting contemporary texts. For instance, a reference stating, "Drake was two and twenty when he obtained the command of the Judith" in 1566, suggests his birth around 1544. Further clues are gleaned from art: a Nicholas Hilliard miniature from 1581 depicts Drake at an alleged age of 42, hinting at a birth year circa 1539, while another portrait from 1594, presenting him as 52 years old, leans towards a birth year around 1541.

Francis was the eldest of twelve sons born to Edmund Drake, a Protestant farmer (1518–1585), and his wife, Mary Mylwaye. The naming of their first son after Francis Russell, the 2nd Earl of Bedford, signifies the family's social connections and aspirations.

The Drake family's life took a dramatic turn during the Prayer Book Rebellion in 1549, compelling them to flee from Devon to Kent due to religious persecution. In Kent, Drake's father secured a significant role as a minister to the men in the King's Navy. His dedication to his faith and service was further cemented when he was ordained a deacon and later appointed as the vicar of Upchurch Church on the Medway. This period of turmoil and relocation played a pivotal role in shaping young Francis Drake's future, setting him on a path that would eventually make him a renowned figure in naval history.

In the mid-16th century, the lucrative West African slave trade was tightly controlled by the Portuguese and Spanish. This monopoly was challenged by Sir John Hawkins, who, with the financial backing of various colleagues and family members, embarked on his inaugural slave trading voyage. Notably absent from this group of investors was Francis Drake, though it's widely believed he participated as a crew member on Hawkins's initial slaving expeditions. Evidence suggests Drake's involvement as a common seaman on the first two voyages, with more concrete proof of his presence on the latter two of Hawkins's four slaving journeys between 1562 and 1569.

Hawkins's first voyage in 1562 was marked by bold actions. He sailed to Sierra Leone, where he captured Portuguese slave ships and sold the captured Africans in the Spanish Indies. The venture proved immensely profitable, prompting a second voyage in 1564 with the support of Queen Elizabeth I herself, who lent him the ship Jesus of Lübeck as his flagship. Hawkins's aggressive strategy continued as he attacked an African town and sold its inhabitants as slaves, generating significant profits for himself, the Queen, and their investors. While Drake was not part of this consortium, he likely received a share of the profits as a crew member. This association later led scholar Kris Lane to list Drake among the first English slave traders.

The Spanish and Portuguese were incensed by the English intrusion into their slave trading domain. Under pressure to prevent an armed conflict, Queen Elizabeth I prohibited Hawkins from undertaking a third slaving voyage.

Undeterred, Hawkins collaborated with his relative John Lovell in 1566 for another voyage, with Drake again on board. This venture, however, ended in failure, with over 90 enslaved Africans being released without payment.

In 1567, Drake joined Hawkins on their final joint venture. Their efforts to capture slaves around Cape Verde were unsuccessful. In Sierra Leone, Hawkins formed an alliance with two local kings, promising assistance against their enemies in exchange for captives. The operation captured several hundred prisoners, but the kings retained the majority, boldly challenging Hawkins's authority.

The fleet's troubles escalated with a series of calamities including storms, Spanish hostility, armed conflict, and a devastating hurricane that separated one of the ships, leaving it to navigate independently back to England. The remaining vessels, in dire need of repairs, were compelled to dock at San Juan de Ulúa near Vera Cruz. However, their respite was short-lived. The new viceroy of New Spain, Martín Enríquez de Almanza, arrived with a fleet, and during negotiations for supplies and repairs, the Spanish launched a surprise attack, leading to the infamous Battle of San Juan de Ulúa.

This battle culminated in a devastating defeat for the English, with most of their ships lost. In a dramatic turn of events, a fireship was sent against Hawkins' flagship, Jesus of Lübeck. Amidst the chaos, the crew of the Minion, in a state of panic, severed their ties with Jesus. Hawkins, in a desperate bid for survival, leapt onto the Minion. Meanwhile, Francis Drake, commanding the Judith, made the fateful decision to flee, leaving Hawkins and others behind. Hawkins, barely escaping on the Minion, endured a harrowing journey back to England, tragically losing many men en route and returning with a mere 15 survivors. This ordeal left hundreds of English sailors abandoned.

Upon his return, Hawkins pointedly accused Drake of desertion and embezzlement. Drake refuted these claims, insisting he had distributed all profits fairly among his crew and believed Hawkins had been lost at sea when he departed.

This tumultuous end to their fourth voyage marked a turning point in Drake's career. From then on, he abandoned slaving and trading, focusing instead on aggressive actions against Spanish interests, fueled by the animosity that had its roots in this fateful battle.

In 1572, Francis Drake launched his first significant solo venture, setting his sights on the Isthmus of Panama, a crucial point for the Spanish Empire. This region, part of Tierra Firme to the Spanish and the Spanish Main to the English, was the key transit point for the immense wealth of Peruvian silver and gold. These treasures were transported overland to the Caribbean Sea, where Spanish galleons at the town of Nombre de Dios would load them for transport to Spain. Departing from Plymouth on May 24, 1572, Drake led a modest crew of 73 men aboard two small ships, the Pascha and the Swan, with the ambitious goal of capturing Nombre de Dios.

Drake's initial assault on Nombre de Dios occurred in late July 1572. Although he successfully took the town, he was severely wounded during a counterattack from Spanish forces from Panama, forcing his men to retreat without securing the treasure. Instead of attacking Nombre de Dios again, Drake shifted his strategy to raiding Spanish galleons along the coast. He also allied with the Cimarrón, escaped African slaves, to raid the mule trains that transported precious goods from Panama City. Among these allies was Diego, who later earned his freedom after serving under Drake.

One of Drake's most renowned exploits on the Spanish Main was the capture of a Spanish silver train at Nombre de Dios on April 1, 1573. This successful raid not only enriched Drake but also significantly boosted his fame. Near Cabo de Cativas, Drake allied with French privateer Guillaume Le Testu, commanding the Havre warship. Together, they planned to intercept a mule train at the Campos River, near Nombre de Dios, and rendezvous with their ships at the Francisca River after the raid. The combined English and French forces, along with Cimarrón scouts, covertly approached the mule train's route. On the morning of April 1, they ambushed the convoy, seizing treasure worth over

200,000 pesos, a fortune at the time.

Following their daring raid on the mule train, Drake and his party found themselves in possession of an astonishing 20 tons of silver and gold. Overwhelmed by the sheer volume of their plunder, they were compelled to bury a significant portion of it, being unable to transport such a vast quantity. They departed with a substantial amount of gold, inadvertently inspiring future legends of pirates and buried treasure. The raid, however, had its costs: the French privateer Le Testu was gravely wounded, captured, and ultimately executed.

The survivors faced a grueling challenge, hauling their precious loot over 18 miles of dense jungle terrain back to their boats, only to discover the boats missing. Stranded, fatigued, and pursued by the Spanish, the situation seemed dire. Yet, Drake's resilience shone through. He motivated his men to bury the treasure on the beach and construct a makeshift raft. Braving the rough seas, they sailed 12 miles to where they had left their pinnaces. Upon reuniting with their crew, Drake, appearing ragged and worn, initially feigned defeat. But soon, revealing a hoard of Spanish gold, he declared triumphantly, "Our voyage is made." By the second week of August 1573, Drake triumphantly returned to Plymouth.

This expedition was also significant for another reason. On February 11, Drake and his lieutenant John Oxenham scaled a high tree in Panama's central mountains, becoming the first Englishmen to lay eyes on the Pacific Ocean, echoing the achievement of Vasco Núñez de Balboa in 1513. Assisted by the Cimarrón leader Pedro, they climbed to a platform atop the tree. Overlooking the vast ocean, they vowed to one day navigate these waters, a promise Drake would fulfill during his world circumnavigation.

Upon Drake's return to England, the political climate was delicate. The government, having signed a truce with Spain's King Philip II, could not openly celebrate Drake's exploits. While hailed as a hero in England, he was branded a pirate in Spain.

In 1575, Drake was involved in a darker episode, the Rathlin Island massacre in Ireland. He, alongside Sir John Norris, acting under the orders of Sir Henry Sidney and the Earl of Essex, Robert Devereux, besieged Rathlin Castle. Despite its surrender, Norris's forces mercilessly killed about 200 defenders and several hundred civilians of Clan MacDonnell. Drake's role was to blockade the island, preventing any Irish or Scottish reinforcements, effectively isolating the leader of the Gaelic resistance, Sorley Boy MacDonnell. This brutal act left Sorley Boy devastated, and it marked a ruthless chapter in the conflict between the English and the Gaelic clans.

In the wake of his Panama isthmus triumph, Sir Francis Drake embarked on the storied "Famous Voyage," a bold campaign targeting Spanish strongholds along the Americas' Pacific coastline. This venture was not just a product of Drake's audacity but also the result of a clandestine alliance with prominent figures like Francis Walsingham, Robert Dudley, Earl of Leicester, John Hawkins, Christopher Hatton, and Drake himself. This alliance was fueled by a plan originally conceived by Sir Richard Grenville. Grenville's vision, initially sanctioned by a royal patent in 1574, faced abrupt disapproval from Queen Elizabeth I upon her realization of its true intent against the Spanish. Yet, in 1577, Drake set sail for South America, possibly with Elizabeth's covert support but without an official commission, embarking on what would become a historic circumnavigation.

Integral to this expedition was Diego, Drake's multilingual assistant, whose fluency in Spanish and English proved invaluable in interactions with captured Spaniards or Portuguese. Diego served not just as an interpreter but also as a full-fledged crew member, earning wages on par with his shipmates. The fleet departed Plymouth on November 15, 1577, but faced immediate peril from severe weather, forcing a retreat to Falmouth for repairs.

Undeterred, Drake relaunched his mission on December 13 aboard the Pelican, leading a fleet of five vessels and 164 men. This fleet soon expanded with the addition of the Mary, a captured Portuguese merchant ship, along with its experienced captain, Nuno da Silva, a navigator well-versed in South American waters.

The voyage was fraught with challenges. Drake had to abandon two ships, the Christopher and the flyboat Swan, due to manpower losses during the Atlantic crossing. The fleet reached the ominous Puerto San Julián in present-day Argentina, a site previously visited by Ferdinand Magellan, where the sight of sun-bleached skeletons on gibbets served as a grim reminder of past mutinies. Echoing Magellan, Drake executed his own perceived mutineer, Thomas Doughty. The Mary, found to be rotting, was stripped and abandoned. Facing these adversities, Drake chose to overwinter in San Julián, preparing for the daunting passage through the Strait of Magellan.

During Sir Francis Drake's daring voyage to disrupt the Spanish treasure fleets, he found himself in escalating disputes with his co-commander, Thomas Doughty. On June 3, 1578, Drake leveled serious accusations against Doughty, charging him with witchcraft, mutiny, and treason during an impromptu trial on board. Drake, asserting he had Queen Elizabeth's authority (though he never produced any formal commission), denied Doughty the opportunity for a trial in England. The key evidence against Doughty came from Edward Bright, the ship's carpenter, whose testimony led to his promotion to master of the Marigold after the trial. Doughty's fate was sealed further by his admission of disclosing the voyage's intentions to Lord Burghley, a known critic of provoking the Spanish.

In a poignant twist, Drake honored Doughty's request for Communion and shared a final meal with him, marked by a mood of sober cheerfulness as recorded by Francis Fletcher. They parted with a toast, under the guise of embarking on a mere journey, not a farewell before an execution.

Tragically, on July 2, 1578, Drake executed Thomas Doughty. Later, in January

1580, while stranded on a reef in the Celebes Sea, Drake's ship's chaplain, Francis Fletcher, suggested in a sermon that their misfortunes were a divine retribution for Doughty's unjust death. In response, Drake excommunicated Fletcher, chaining him as a sign of his displeasure.

Meanwhile, the fleet, now reduced to three ships, continued towards the Magellan Strait. There, in September 1578, violent storms led to the loss of the Marigold, captained by John Thomas, and forced the Elizabeth, under John Wynter, to turn back to England. Only the Pelican, Drake's flagship, made it through to the Pacific. In this part of the journey, Drake and his crew faced extreme southern latitudes, possibly reaching 55°S along the Chilean coast, as noted in Richard Hakluyt's "The Principall Navigations."

Drake's interactions with the indigenous populations in southern Patagonia were marked by violence, resulting in the first European-inflicted casualties in that region. It was also here that his crew discovered the anti-scurvy properties of the bark of Drimys winteri, a discovery credited to Captain Wynter.

Historian Mateo Martinic's examination of Drake's records highlights his significant discovery of the southern end of the Americas and the oceanic space beyond it. This recognition of Drake's navigational achievements only came into the spotlight following the 1618 publication of Willem Schouten and Jacob le Maire's voyage around Cape Horn in 1616.

On his remarkable voyage, Sir Francis Drake continued his journey aboard his flagship, now rechristened the Golden Hind in tribute to his patron Sir Christopher Hatton, whose coat of arms featured a golden hind. The Golden Hind navigated northward along the Pacific coast of South America, boldly raiding Spanish ports and seizing towns. Drake's encounters with Spanish vessels not only resulted in their capture but also provided him with superior navigation charts.

One significant incident occurred near Mocha Island, now part of Chile, where Drake and his manservant Diego were gravely injured by the Mapuche people's arrows. Undeterred, Drake proceeded to Valparaíso in Chile, where he successfully plundered the port and captured a ship laden with Chilean wine.

Near Lima, Drake's fortunes soared with the capture of a Spanish ship carrying 25,000 pesos in Peruvian gold, equivalent to about 37,000 ducats in Spanish currency or roughly £7 million by today's standards. Additionally, Drake learned of the Nuestra Señora de la Concepción, a treasure-laden ship bound for Manila, soon to be known as Cacafuego. After a determined pursuit, Drake captured this vessel, marking his most lucrative prize.

Aboard the Nuestra Señora de la Concepción, Drake discovered an astonishing treasure: 36 kilograms of gold, a golden crucifix, jewels, 13 chests of silver reals, and 26,000 kilograms of silver. Celebrating this windfall, Drake dined with the captured ship's officers and gentleman passengers, later releasing them with gifts befitting their rank and letters of safe conduct.

Drake's journey northward was marked by more raids on Spanish settlements and ships. His final major stop was in Guatulco, where his crew plundered provisions from April 13 to 16. Contemplating his return to England, Drake faced a strategic decision: to avoid the perilous Strait of Magellan and the likely Spanish opposition along the coast, he had to choose between seeking a rumored northern passage, the Strait of Anián, or undertaking an audacious circumnavigation of the globe by crossing the Pacific to the East Indies and then back to England.

In May, Sir Francis Drake and his crew, aboard their two ships, ventured past the Baja Peninsula, pressing northwards. Prior to this journey, the western coast of North America had seen limited exploration, most notably by Juan Rodríguez Cabrillo in 1542 on behalf of Spain. Drake, keen to steer clear of Spanish territories, navigated northwest, searching for a secluded spot to ready his crew for their return to England.

The exact northern reach of Drake's expedition along this coast has been a topic of much historical debate, but the consensus is that he achieved a latitude of at least 48° north before deciding to head south again.

On June 5, 1579, Drake's ship first touched land at what is today known as South Cove, Cape Arago, just south of Coos Bay, Oregon. Continuing southward, on June 17, they discovered a sheltered cove along the Pacific coast of what is now Northern California. Here, Drake claimed the land for Queen Elizabeth I, naming it Nova Albion, or New Albion. He left an engraved brass plate to assert England's sovereignty. The crew spent several weeks ashore, fortifying their position and repairing the Golden Hind by careening it to clean and fix its hull.

Drake and his crew had cordial encounters with the local Coast Miwok people and explored the area. Setting off again on July 23, they made a brief stop at the Farallon Islands for hunting sea lions or seals.

Leaving the Pacific coast, Drake headed southwest to catch the winds for crossing the Pacific. A few months later, he arrived at the Moluccas, a group of islands in today's eastern Indonesia. Contrary to some scholarly views, Harry Kelsey suggests that Drake may have actually prepared his ship at Magdalena Bay in Lower California before heading to the Moluccas and Spice Islands.

During this leg of the voyage, Drake's manservant Diego succumbed to earlier sustained wounds. The Golden Hind narrowly escaped disaster after getting trapped on a reef. The crew had to wait for favorable tides and even jettisoned some cargo. In the Moluccas, Drake befriended Sultan Babullah of Ternate, getting entangled in local politics with the Portuguese.

The journey continued with multiple stops en route to Africa, rounding the

Cape of Good Hope, and finally reaching Sierra Leone by July 22, 1580, marking the final stages of this historic circumnavigation.

On September 26, 1580, the Golden Hind triumphantly returned to Plymouth, captained by Drake with 59 of his crew, laden with a rich bounty of spices and captured Spanish treasures. The wealth acquired was so immense that the Queen's share alone exceeded the total income of the Crown for that entire year. Drake's achievement was celebrated as he became the first Englishman to complete a circumnavigation of the Earth, the second successful such voyage since Elcano's in 1520 with at least one ship returning intact.

In an effort to maintain an element of secrecy over Drake's exploits and to protect them from Spanish eyes, Queen Elizabeth ordered that all written accounts of his voyages be classified as state secrets. Drake and his associates were sworn to silence under penalty of death, highlighting the delicate political context of his achievements.

Among the treasures Drake brought back was a remarkable jewel token, a testament to his circumnavigation. Crafted from enamelled gold, adorned with an African diamond and featuring a ship with an ebony hull, it was a prize from the Pacific coast of Mexico presented to the Queen.

In gratitude for his services, Queen Elizabeth bestowed upon Drake an extraordinary gift: the Drake Jewel. This lavish pendant, encrusted with diamonds, rubies, and pearls, was a significant honor for a commoner. Captured in a 1591 portrait by Marcus Gheeraerts, this jewel featured a state portrait of Elizabeth by miniaturist Nicholas Hilliard on one side and a sardonyx cameo on the other. The cameo portrayed regal and African male busts. The Drake Jewel, a rare sixteenth-century artifact, is now preserved at the Victoria and Albert Museum in London.

Drake's knighthood was conferred on April 4, 1581, aboard the Golden Hind in Deptford. In a strategic political move, the ceremony was performed by Monsieur de Marchaumont, a French diplomat involved in matrimonial negotiations between Elizabeth and Francis, Duke of Anjou, brother of the King of France. This involvement of a French diplomat subtly garnered French support for Drake's activities, a clever maneuver by Queen Elizabeth. Contrary to later Victorian narratives that romantically claimed Elizabeth herself performed the knighting, it was, in fact, a diplomatic affair.

Drake also claimed a coat of arms from the ancient Devon family of Drake of Ash, alleging distant kinship. When this right was legally challenged, Queen Elizabeth granted Drake his own coat of arms, a testament to his elevated status. The heraldic achievement embodied the motto "Sic Parvis Magna," meaning "Great achievements from small beginnings," and featured a hand emerging from clouds with the inscription "Auxilio Divino," translating to "By divine aid," signifying the providential aspect of his voyages.

Sir Francis Drake's political and naval career was as dynamic as his voyages. He first entered the political arena as a member of parliament representing Camelford in the final session of Elizabeth I's 4th Parliament, starting January 16, 1581. His parliamentary duties, however, were brief at this time, as he was soon granted leave on February 17, 1581, for urgent matters related to the Queen's service.

In September 1581, Drake's influence extended to local governance when he became the Mayor of Plymouth. His mayoral tenure was marked by notable civic contributions, including the installation of a compass at Plymouth Hoe and the enactment of regulations for the local pilchard fishery. Moreover, Drake's entrepreneurial spirit was evident in his construction of a leat, or canal, from the River Meavy, alongside six new gristmills, which turned out to be quite profitable.

Drake re-entered parliament in 1584, this time representing Bossiney in the 5th Parliament of Elizabeth I. His active participation in this parliamentary term focused on naval matters, fishing, early American colonization, and issues pertinent to Devon. However, his parliamentary duties were interrupted by other commitments, including an expedition to Portugal.

By 1593, Drake was representing Plymouth in parliament, where he vigorously advocated for issues relevant to Plymouth, particularly those concerning defense against Spain.

The outbreak of war between England and Spain in 1585, following the Treaty of Nonsuch, saw Drake's return to military action. Under orders from Queen Elizabeth I and her principal secretary Francis Walsingham, Drake led a pre-emptive strike against Spanish colonies. Setting sail from Plymouth in September 1585 with a fleet of twenty-one ships and 1,800 soldiers under Christopher Carleill, he first targeted Vigo in Spain, followed by Santiago in the Cape Verde Islands. The expedition then crossed the Atlantic, raiding Santo Domingo, and capturing Cartagena de Indias in modern-day Colombia, where he notably freed a hundred enslaved Turks.

On June 6, 1586, Drake attacked and destroyed the Spanish fort at San Agustín in Florida. He also played a crucial role in aiding Sir Walter Raleigh's Roanoke settlement, providing supplies and returning with the original colonists before the arrival of Sir Richard Grenville with additional supplies and settlers.

Drake's return to England on July 22 was met with a hero's welcome as he sailed into Portsmouth, having firmly established himself as a key figure in England's maritime and political history.

To counter the increasing threat from English and Dutch privateers, including the likes of Sir Francis Drake, against its interests in the Americas, King Philip II of Spain orchestrated a grand plan to invade England.

On March 15, 1587, Drake received a new commission with multiple objectives. His mission was to disrupt the vital supply routes from Italy and Andalucia to Lisbon, harass Spanish fleets in their home ports, and capture treasure-laden

Spanish ships. Additionally, Drake was tasked to engage the Spanish Armada if it had already embarked towards England.

Drake arrived at Cádiz on April 19, 1587, to find the harbor brimming with ships and supplies, as the Armada was gearing up for its expedition against England. Seizing the opportunity, Drake launched a daring attack in the early hours of the following day, causing significant damage within the inner harbor. The extent of Spanish losses varies in different accounts: Drake claimed to have sunk 39 ships, while the Spanish acknowledged the loss of 24. This bold assault, famously dubbed as the "singeing of the King's beard," effectively delayed the Spanish invasion by a year.

In the subsequent month, Drake's fleet patrolled the coasts between Lisbon and Cape St. Vincent. They successfully intercepted and destroyed numerous ships, disrupting the Spanish supply lines. Drake estimated that his fleet had captured about 1,600 to 1,700 tons of barrel staves, sufficient to make 25,000 to 30,000 barrels for storing provisions. The financial outcome of this expedition was substantial for England, yielding a total profit of around £140,000, of which £18,235 was awarded to Drake himself.

In May 1588, the formidable Spanish Armada embarked on its mission to invade England, arriving off the Cornish coast on July 29. The English, prepared to defend their shores, dispatched a fleet of 55 ships from Plymouth under the command of Lord Howard of Effingham. Sir Francis Drake, serving as vice admiral aboard the galleon Revenge, played a pivotal role in the ensuing confrontations.

As night fell and the English fleet pursued the Armada up the Channel, Drake seized an opportunity to capture the Spanish galleon Nuestra Señora del Rosario. The galleon, under the command of Admiral Pedro de Valdés, was known to be carrying significant funds for the Armada. Drake's tactical maneuver, which involved extinguishing his ship's guiding lantern, momentarily threw the English fleet into confusion but ultimately resulted in a significant prize.

The Spanish fleet, commanded by the inexperienced Duke of Medina Sidonia, navigated towards Calais, believing the English would not dare attack them in French territorial waters.

A decisive strategy emerged during a council of war aboard Howard's flagship, Ark. The English leaders, including Howard, Drake, Seymour, Hawkins, and Martin Frobisher, decided to deploy fire ships against the anchored Spanish fleet. This bold move on the night of the attack forced the Spanish to hastily depart from Calais, leading to a crucial engagement off the shoals of Gravelines. Here, Drake and his compatriots, including Frobisher and Hawkins, fiercely bombarded the Spanish ships. Although the Spanish flagship San Martin, heavily engaged by Frobisher, survived the onslaught, five Spanish ships were lost in the battle.

Drake, aboard the Revenge, described the intensity of the confrontation in a letter to Admiral Henry Seymour, noting the determination of the Spanish to fiercely defend themselves.

Following their failure to achieve their objective and unable to return via the English Channel, the remnants of the Armada were compelled to navigate around the British Isles. Harsh storms off the Irish coast further ravaged the Spanish fleet, leading to substantial losses as they eventually returned to Spain.

Amidst these historical events, a famous, albeit likely apocryphal, story emerged about Drake. It is said that while playing bowls on Plymouth Hoe, he was informed of the approaching Spanish Armada. Drake allegedly remarked that there was enough time to finish the game before confronting the Spanish, suggesting a confident, if cavalier, attitude. This story, first recorded 37 years after the event, likely stems from the English fleet's delay caused by adverse winds and currents as the Spanish neared, contributing to the myth of Drake's nonchalant approach to the Spanish threat.

In 1589, a year after the Spanish Armada's defeat, England launched its own counter-offensive against Spain. Sir Francis Drake and Sir John Norris were assigned three critical objectives: to destroy the remnants of the Spanish Atlantic fleet undergoing repairs in northern Spain, to incite a rebellion in Lisbon, Portugal against King Philip II (also Philip I of Portugal), and to install the claimant Dom António, Prior of Crato, on the Portuguese throne. Additionally, they were tasked with capturing the Azores, if possible, to establish a permanent English base.

The campaign began with an assault on Coruña, Spain, where Drake and Norris managed to destroy some ships in the harbor but ultimately faced a repelling force. This setback cost them two weeks, forcing them to abandon the pursuit of the surviving Spanish ships and proceed directly to Lisbon.

Norris led a grueling overland march to Lisbon, while Drake navigated around the peninsula, planning to rendezvous with the Earl of Essex and his artillery. By the time Norris's troops reached Lisbon, they were exhausted and sick. Norris demanded local support for Dom António's cause, threatening to retreat otherwise. Contrary to their plan, Drake anchored his fleet at the Tagus estuary's mouth, avoiding the heavily fortified stretches of the river and failing to deliver the critical heavy artillery.

The anticipated Portuguese uprising never materialized, and the ground operation in Lisbon ended in failure. Norris, along with his army and António, retreated, attempting to capture the Spanish treasure fleet. Adverse weather, however, forced them to abandon this plan and return to England.

Drake, seeking to salvage the mission's reputation, made a brief stop in Galicia, Spain. He pillaged and razed the town of Vigo, but this act of desperation resulted in significant losses, with hundreds of men killed or wounded. As local defenses strengthened and Portuguese militias arrived,

Drake's fleet had to retreat. Two English vessels were later captured by a Spanish squadron led by Captain Diego de Aramburu in the Bay of Biscay.

The expedition's failure was costly, with estimates of English casualties ranging from 8,000 to over 20,000 soldiers and sailors. Upon his return, Drake faced scrutiny and criticism for his conduct and decisions during the expedition. The Privy Council charged him with mismanagement and failures, leading to a significant decline in his favor. As a result, Drake did not receive command of another naval expedition until 1595.

Sir Francis Drake's illustrious career as a mariner extended into his mid-fifties, marked by both daring exploits and notable setbacks. In 1595, his ambitions suffered a blow when he failed to capture the port of Las Palmas. This disappointment was followed by a series of defeats in his campaign against Spanish America. During an unsuccessful assault on San Juan de Puerto Rico, Drake narrowly escaped death when a cannonball from El Morro Castle tore through his flagship's stateroom.

Drake, along with his second-in-command Thomas Baskerville, managed to capture and burn the town of Nombre de Dios. They then embarked on an overland expedition to seize Panama City. However, this venture was thwarted by well-prepared Spanish defenses, who had barricaded the approach roads. Facing heavy casualties, Drake and his men were forced to abandon their plan.

Tragically, on January 28, 1596, Drake succumbed to dysentery, a rampant disease in the tropics during that era, while his fleet was anchored off the coast of Portobelo, where Spanish treasure ships had taken refuge. His death, at approximately 56 years of age, led to the withdrawal of the English fleet in defeat.

In his final moments, Drake expressed a wish to be dressed in his full armor. Respecting his last request, he was laid to rest at sea in a lead-lined coffin, near the coast of Portobelo. His burial site is believed to be in the vicinity of the sunken British ships Elizabeth and Delight in Portobelo Bay. Despite ongoing efforts by researchers and treasure hunters, the exact location of Drake's underwater grave remains undiscovered, with divers continuing to scour the seabed in hopes of finding his coffin.

Pedro Menéndez de Avilés

P edro Menéndez de Avilés' life story unfolds like a captivating historical drama, deeply rooted in the rich tapestry of 16th-century Spain. Born into the distinguished and noble family of Juan Alonso Sánchez de Avilés and María Alonso y Menéndez Arango in the regal Kingdom of Asturias, Pedro was one of the youngest in a large brood of twenty siblings. His early life was marked by the pivotal War of Granada, where his father bravely served the Catholic Monarchs, shaping the backdrop of Pedro's upbringing.

Tragedy struck early in Pedro's life when his father passed away, leaving a young Pedro and his siblings under the care of their mother, Doña Maria. The family dynamics took another turn when Doña Maria remarried, leading to a crucial decision to send Pedro away to live with a relative. This relative, tasked with overseeing his education and upbringing, soon found himself at odds with the strong-willed and spirited Pedro. This friction eventually led Pedro to make a bold and rash decision: he ran away from his foster home, seeking independence and adventure.

Pedro's disappearance stirred concern and after an extensive search, he was found six months later in the bustling city of Valladolid. Despite being returned to his foster home, the seeds of rebellion and a thirst for adventure had been firmly planted in him. It wasn't long before Pedro's destiny steered him towards a military career, a path that promised both honor and challenges.

His early military ventures saw him joining forces to combat the French corsairs, who were notorious for disrupting Spain's maritime commerce. Serving at sea in a modest armada, Pedro began to carve out a name for himself, demonstrating both bravery and tactical acumen.

After two years of intense combat, Pedro Menéndez de Avilés, emboldened by his experiences, returned home with a visionary plan. Fueled by his newfound ambition and a portion of his family inheritance, he set out to construct his very own vessel. The result was a patache, a small yet swift and agile row-sailer, perfectly designed for the rigorous demands of coastal patrol. This vessel wasn't just a means of transportation; it was the embodiment of Menéndez's bold aspirations for maritime adventure.

With his patache ready, Menéndez began assembling a crew, primarily consisting of his own relatives, all eager to join him in his quest for adventure and glory on the high seas. This tight-knit crew shared a common bond of kinship and a collective thirst for the unknown, making them a formidable force on the waters.

The young Menéndez quickly proved his mettle as a commander during a fierce confrontation with French corsairs. These pirates had ambushed three slow-moving Spanish freighters off the rugged coast of Galicia. Demonstrating exceptional strategic acumen and captainship, Menéndez masterfully outmaneuvered two nimble zabras that were in hot pursuit, capturing them both in a stunning display of naval prowess. He also successfully repelled the third assailant, marking a significant victory in his burgeoning maritime career.

This remarkable feat catapulted Menéndez into the limelight, making him a subject of widespread admiration and discussion among the maritime communities of both Spain and France. His name resonated through the corridors of royal courts, heralding him as a rising star on the maritime stage. However, his escalating fame and influence did not sit well with everyone.

The merchants of Seville and the influential Casa de Contrataciónviewed Menéndez's successes with a mix of awe and apprehension. His growing clout with the Spanish Crown, particularly due to his naval exploits, began to stir a sense of unease among these established commercial powers.

Pedro Menéndez de Avilés is renowned for his pioneering role in surveying and authorizing the construction of royal fortresses at key Caribbean ports. In 1554, in a move that underscored his growing prominence, the Spanish Crown appointed him as Captain-General of the Fleet of the Indies, the prestigious Spanish treasure fleet. That year marked a notable achievement in his career as he led the fleet on a successful voyage, ensuring its safe return to Spain. This appointment was a departure from the norm, as traditionally, the influential Casa de Contratación had overseen such positions.

Menéndez's strategic insight was evident in his emphasis on the significance of the Bahama Channel and his recognition of Havana, Cuba, as a crucial port for the annual rendezvous of the treasure-laden Flota galleons. This strategic vision and his successes in maritime ventures fostered a close relationship with King Philip II of Spain. This bond was further cemented when Menéndez was invited to join the Royal Party during Philip's marriage to Mary I of England.

In 1559, Philip II reaffirmed his trust in Menéndez by reappointing him as Captain General of the Fleet of the Indies, with his brother Bartolomé Menéndez serving as Admiral. That October, Menéndez embarked for the Indies, commanding the galleons of the grand Armada de la Carrera, or Spanish Treasure Fleet. His leadership was instrumental in navigating the fleet's return voyage from the Caribbean and Mexico to Spain, skillfully utilizing the Florida Strait and leveraging the Gulf Stream current.

However, Menéndez's career was not without challenges. In 1561, he faced allegations of smuggling by Casa officials, leading to his imprisonment. Determinedly, he managed to have his case transferred to court, where he successfully secured his release.

Menéndez's legacy also includes his vital role in the establishment of the Spanish treasure fleet convoy system, which became the lifeline between Spain and its overseas territories. Collaborating with Álvaro de Bazán, the 1st Marquis of Santa Cruz, he contributed to the design of the majestic galleons that facilitated trade between Cadiz in Spain and Vera Cruz in Spanish Mexico.

In his later years, as adelantado, Menéndez was tasked with exploring a vast territory stretching from the Gulf coast of present-day western Florida to Newfoundland. He was also instructed by the king to establish several fortified presidios, populate them with settlers and slaves, and initiate the conversion of the Indigenous peoples to Catholicism, marking his role as not just a military leader but also a key figure in the Spanish colonial expansion.

In 1562, an event occurred that would significantly impact the Spanish claim to La Florida. A group of French Huguenots, led by Jean Ribault, arrived in this Spanish-claimed territory. They explored the St. Johns River in Florida, naming it 'la Rivière de Mai' (the River May), and then moved north to establish a settlement they called Charlesfort, located at Port Royal Sound in what is now South Carolina.

Meanwhile, in August 1563, Pedro Menéndez and his brother Bartolomé found themselves embroiled in legal troubles. They were imprisoned by the Casa de Contratación on charges of bribery and smuggling silver into Spain. While incarcerated, Menéndez received the distressing news of the disappearance of La Concepción, the flagship of the New Spain fleet, which was commanded by his son, Admiral Juan Menéndez. The ship was presumed lost, along with all hands, during a hurricane off the coast of South Carolina near Bermuda.

Amidst this personal and professional crisis, Menéndez hatched a plan to venture to La Florida in search of his son, whom he hoped might have survived. However, his imprisonment rendered him powerless to act on this plan, and his pleas for assistance to King Philip II went unanswered.

Spain, vigilant of its territorial claims, became aware of the French expedition to Florida through its intelligence network. Philip II was particularly alarmed upon learning that Jean Ribault had been appointed as the "Captain-General and Viceroy of New France" and was preparing a significant expedition in Dieppe. This expedition, aimed at strengthening French presence in Florida, reportedly consisted of over 500 arquebusiers and several bronze cannons.

After his eventual release from prison, Menéndez was once again available to serve the Spanish Crown. He was appointed adelantado of La Florida, a position that came with the promise of a substantial land grant and the title of marquis upon successful completion of his duties. Menéndez advised King Philip II of the strategic value in exploring the Florida coast, not only for potential trade routes to China and the Molucca Islands but also as a means to access the mines of New Spain in central Mexico and to reach the Pacific. He proposed the colonization of several areas within Florida to defend against both the native populations and foreign intrusions.

Driven by both personal ambition and a commitment to enhance the wealth of the Spanish royal treasury, he had grand plans for his Florida venture. He envisioned a prosperous enterprise encompassing agriculture, fisheries, and naval stores. Crucially, his ambitious undertaking was backed by a robust network of seventeen northern Spanish families, all linked through blood and marriage. These families, sharing Menéndez's vision, pledged their resources and fortunes to the adelantado, anticipating future rewards in the form of extensive land grants and esteemed royal honors in civil and military positions in La Florida. This alliance provided Menéndez with a cadre of loyal lieutenants and officials, bound to him by kinship and a shared stake in his success.

In early 1564, Menéndez sought permission from the Crown to travel to Florida. His primary aim was to search for La Concepcion and his son,

Admiral Juan Menéndez, who had commanded the vessel before it was lost in a hurricane in 1563. However, his requests continued to be denied by the Crown.

Meanwhile, René de Laudonnière, a Huguenot noble who had been part of Jean Ribault's initial expedition, returned to Florida in 1564 with three ships and 300 colonists. On June 22, 1564, he arrived at the River May, where he founded Fort Caroline just a few miles upstream. This French settlement in such close proximity to the Spanish treasure fleet's route deeply concerned the Spanish Crown.

In response to these European encroachments on its claimed territories in North America, the Spanish Crown empowered Menéndez with a significant asiento. Signed by Philip II on March 20, 1565, this agreement granted Menéndez extensive trade rights, the authority to distribute lands, licenses to sell up to 500 slaves, and various titles, including adelantado of Florida. His mission was to conduct a thorough reconnaissance of North America, from the Florida Keys to modern-day Canada, documenting coastal features and establishing a permanent settlement to defend the Spanish treasure fleet. Additionally, Menéndez was tasked with expelling any non-Spanish intruders, further solidifying Spain's claim to the region.

On 28 July 1565, Pedro Menéndez de Avilés embarked on a significant voyage from Cádiz. Leading his fleet was the 600-ton flagship San Pelayo, accompanied by several smaller vessels. This formidable flotilla, carrying over 1,000 individuals including sailors, soldiers, and settlers, was a clear statement of Spain's colonial ambitions in the New World.

The fleet made landfall on 28 August, coinciding with the feast day of St. Augustine, near a tidal channel the French had named the River of Dolphins. This area would later be developed into what is now known as the city of St. Augustine. Menéndez wasted no time in asserting his presence, engaging in a brief naval skirmish with Jean Ribault's fleet near the River May. On 6

September, after returning to his initial landing site, Menéndez named it St. Augustine in honor of the saint, disembarked his forces, and quickly set about building fortifications.

The historical significance of this moment was marked by Father Francisco López de Mendoza Grajales, the expedition's chaplain, who celebrated the first Thanksgiving Mass on American soil. This event led to the establishment of Mission Nombre de Dios at the landing site, arguably the first mission in what would become the continental United States. The mission played a vital role in the region, serving the Mocama, a Timucua group, and forming the heart of an influential chiefdom in the late 16th and 17th centuries.

Menéndez then turned his attention to the French Huguenots at Fort Caroline, situated on the St. Johns River. In a surprise attack on 20 September 1565, his forces overran the fort, sparing only the women and children but killing 132 Frenchmen. The fort was subsequently claimed for Spain and renamed San Mateo. In a later act of retaliation in 1568, French soldiers would return to destroy this fort, killing the Spanish garrison.

Meanwhile, Jean Ribault had set out with four ships to attack St. Augustine but was caught in a violent storm. The storm wrecked three of his ships near what is now Ponce de Leon Inlet, with his flagship running aground near present-day Cape Canaveral. Menéndez, informed by local Native American allies of the French survivors' location, began a search and eventually found them near the Matanzas River's southern entrance. Following negotiations, Ribault and his men, numbering between 150 and 350, surrendered to the Spanish. In a brutal act that would give the area its name, Matanzas (Spanish for "slaughters"), nearly all the French captives were executed by the Spanish.

Having secured control of the Florida coast, Menéndez focused on completing the fort at St. Augustine. He also initiated missions for the Catholic Church among the native populations and conducted explorations along the east coast and interior of the Florida peninsula.

In May 1566, amidst escalating tensions with the neighboring Timucua Indians, Pedro Menéndez de Avilés took decisive action to safeguard the Spanish settlement. He relocated it to a more defensible location on the northern end of a barrier island, strategically positioned between the mainland and the sea, where he constructed a wooden fort. By 1572, seeking even greater security and stability, the settlement was moved again, this time to the mainland, just south of what would become the town plaza. As governor, Menéndez not only fortified this new position but also embarked on explorations to strengthen the region's defenses further.

In addition to his efforts in fortifying the settlement, Menéndez commissioned an ambitious expedition under the leadership of Captain Juan Pardo. This expedition, starting from Santa Elena at Port Royal Sound in present-day South Carolina, was tasked with an extraordinary mission: to find an overland route to the Spanish silver mines in central Mexico. The Spanish, under a geographical misconception, believed the Appalachian Mountains were part of a mountain range that extended to Mexico. Over the next few years, Pardo's expedition ventured into present-day South Carolina and Western North Carolina. They reached the Mississippian chiefdom of Joara, where they established Fort San Juan and spent the winter. In total, Pardo's team built six forts along this route, including San Pedro at Olamico in southeastern Tennessee, near the principal town of the Chiaha chiefdom.

However, Pardo's expedition faced a grim end. By 1568, Native American resistance, fueled by opposition to the Spanish presence and their treatment, led to the death of all but one of the Spanish soldiers in the garrisons, and the destruction of the forts. This marked the end of Spanish attempts to colonize this interior region.

Having successfully established and fortified settlements along the coast of La Florida, Menéndez returned to Spain in 1567, confident in having fulfilled his contract with the King. His achievements earned him the appointment as the governor of Cuba in October of that year. Menéndez continued to travel across the Atlantic, but his health began to deteriorate.

Pedro Menéndez de Avilés embarked on a journey to southwest Florida, driven by the hope of finding his son. During this quest, he encountered the Calusa tribe, known for their maritime prowess, in the region of present-day Charlotte Harbor. Menéndez initiated a peace treaty with the Calusa leader, Carlos, a peace further cemented by his marriage to Carlos's sister, who upon baptism was named Doña Antonia. However, the alliance was fragile. Menéndez's strategy of using Doña Antonia as a bargaining chip in his negotiations with the Calusas, coupled with his dealings with their rivals, the Tocobagas, ultimately led to a deterioration in relations, sparking a prolonged and intermittent war that lasted into the next century. Despite these efforts, his son Juan remained untraceable.

Menéndez then established a Spanish garrison up the coast and proceeded to explore the Georgia coast, making contact with the indigenous people of St. Catherines Island. Returning to Florida, he expanded Spanish influence across southeastern Florida, building additional fortifications and reinforcing his position as governor. In 1567, his journey took him south to encounter the Ais (Jece) near the Indian River, in the vicinity of modern-day Vero Beach. Later that year, he returned to Spain and was appointed governor of Cuba in October.

In December 1571, Menéndez faced a perilous situation when a storm wrecked his vessel at Cape Canaveral while sailing from Florida to Havana. He miraculously survived, reaching the fort of St. Augustine with seventeen companions. During this journey, he adeptly avoided attacks by the Ais tribe, using his wits and strategic threats to deter them. The Ais, along with other tribes like the Tequesta and Calusa, continued to resist Spanish settlement, with conflicts persisting until 1670.

Menéndez also established contact with the less hostile Tequesta tribe at their capital in El Portal (now Miami). He managed to negotiate with them to provide three chieftains as translators to the Arawak during a trip to Cuba. Despite leaving Jesuit missionaries Brother Francisco de Villareal and Padre Rogel to convert the Tequesta to Roman Catholicism, the tribe showed little interest, leading the Jesuits to return to St. Augustine after a year.

Menéndez's final voyage to La Florida occurred in 1571, bringing 650 settlers to Santa Elena, accompanied by his wife and family. In August 1572, he led an expedition to avenge the deaths of Jesuits in the Ajacán Mission in present-day Virginia. His life's journey culminated with his appointment as governor of Cuba shortly after arriving there. Pedro Menéndez de Avilés passed away from typhus in Santander, Spain, on 17 September 1574, leaving behind a complex legacy of exploration, colonial administration, and cultural encounters.

Thomas Cavendish

Thomas Cavendish's life, baptized on 19th September 1560 in the historic St Martin's Church in Trimley St Martin, Suffolk, unfolds like a captivating tale from an old English chronicle. He was the third son in the lineage of William Cavendish and Mary Wentworth, a family of considerable standing. The early demise of his father in 1572 marked a turning point in young Cavendish's life, as he inherited a substantial estate. This inheritance brought him under the guardianship of Thomas Wentworth, 2nd Baron Wentworth, a figure of notable influence, who was tasked with the crucial responsibility of preparing him for a university education.

In the vibrant spring of 1576, at the tender age of 15, Cavendish embarked on his academic journey at Corpus Christi College, Cambridge. This period at Cambridge was short-lived, as he departed in November 1577 without earning a degree, an unusual move for someone of his standing. Following this, Cavendish entered Gray's Inn in London, a decision that marked a new chapter in his life. It was here, amidst the grandeur and complexity of London society, that he carved out a lavish lifestyle for himself, rubbing shoulders with influential figures at the royal court.

During these formative years in London, Cavendish's path crossed with that of Richard Hakluyt and others who were fervent proponents of English colonization in North America. These interactions ignited in him a sense of adventure and a keen interest in the world beyond England's shores. However, alongside his rising social stature, Cavendish also gained notoriety as a spendthrift. His extravagant lifestyle led him down a path of financial recklessness, culminating in a series of court cases between 1583 and 1585 over his failure to settle debts.

In the bustling decade of the 1580s, Thomas Cavendish ambitiously sought advancement through the patronage of the notable Walter Raleigh. Raleigh, along with the Earl of Pembroke, played a pivotal role in Cavendish's ascent to political prominence, assisting him in securing a seat in the House of Commons as a member of parliament for Shaftesbury in 1584. This newfound political stature allowed Cavendish to champion Raleigh's endeavors, notably Raleigh's ambitious plans to take over Humphrey Gilbert's contract for American colonization. Furthering his maritime knowledge, Cavendish diligently studied navigation under the expert guidance of Thomas Harriot at Raleigh's esteemed Durham House in Westminster.

1585 marked a significant year in Cavendish's life. He was appointed as the deputy to Richard Grenville in a daring expedition aimed at establishing the Roanoke Colony in Virginia. Demonstrating his commitment, Cavendish invested heavily in the fleet's purchase and provisioning, a testament to his dedication to the colonial cause. Departing Plymouth on the 9th of April 1585, the fleet encountered a fierce storm, scattering the ships. However, Cavendish, aboard the ship Elizabeth, showcased his navigational prowess by surviving the tempest and reaching the designated rendezvous point in Puerto Rico, much to Grenville's admiration.

The Caribbean became their temporary base as Grenville and Cavendish spent several weeks amassing supplies essential for the nascent colony. They engaged in complex interactions with the Spanish in Hispaniola, purchasing supplies and even seizing two Spanish ships encountered during their voyage. Finally, in late June, they arrived at the Outer Banks in what is now North Carolina, marking the spot for the establishment of the Roanoke Colony.

Cavendish's return to England in August aboard the Tyger was not laden with the expected profits from his investments. Nonetheless, the voyage was far from fruitless. It endowed him with invaluable experience, a deeper understanding of the complexities of maritime expeditions, and the forging of several enduring friendships.

On the 21st of July 1586, Thomas Cavendish embarked from Plymouth Sound with a fleet of three ships, setting sail on an expedition that would etch his name in the annals of maritime history. Merely five days into their voyage, near Cape Finisterre, Cavendish and his fleet found themselves engaged in a distant, long-range skirmish with five Biscayne ships. This encounter, spanning nearly three hours, ended only with the veil of darkness, allowing them to lose contact and proceed.

Their journey took them past the Canary Islands, eventually reaching the coast of present-day Sierra Leone on the 21st of August. Here, they spent eleven days gathering provisions and water. During this time, Cavendish's crew interacted with the local inhabitants, engaging in cultural exchanges that included dances and night festivities. A plan to capture a Portuguese ship, marred by miscommunication with the locals, led to an unintended burning of a native village and a hasty retreat with minimal loot. The natives' response was swift, launching poisoned arrows, one of which fatally wounded an English sailor.

In early September, Cavendish and his fleet left the African shores, crossing the Atlantic towards Portuguese Brazil. After a brief stop in the Cape Verde Islands for water, they reached an island off São Sebastião on November 1, 1586. Here, they constructed a pinnace and replenished their water supplies before venturing further south.

By mid-December, Cavendish had navigated down the South American East coast, discovering an estuary with a suitable harbor, which he named Port Desire after his flagship. The only inhabitants were a few Native Americans, whose arrow attacks resulted in injuries to some crew members. Finding scant fresh water, Cavendish continued onward, reaching the Strait of Magellan on January 6, 1587, amidst heavy swells from an approaching storm.

In the Strait of Magellan, Cavendish's vessels navigated through Segunda Angostura, the narrowest part of the straits, and anchored at Santa Magdalena Island. There, in a mere two hours, they hunted and salted enough penguins to fill two barrels for sustenance. Further along, they encountered the remnants of Rey don Felipe, a settlement established by Pedro Sarmiento de Gamboa. Astonishingly, only fifteen survivors remained from the original 400 Spanish settlers. Cavendish, in a merciless decision, offered no aid except to Tomé Hernandez, a veteran pilot he intended to utilize. He seized six cannons and grimly renamed the place 'Port Famine'.

Continuing through the second half of the strait, Cavendish embarked on extensive exploration of the inlets, channels, and fragmented landscapes of Tierra del Fuego and its surrounding areas. Emerging into the Pacific on February 24, 1587, they sailed north along the western coast of South America.

During his voyage, Cavendish and his fleet encountered a formidable storm that steered them further north and separated the Hugh Gallant from the other ships. For almost four grueling days, the tempest raged, rendering sleep impossible for the weary sailors. Eventually, on March 15, 1587, they arrived at Santa María Island. There, a landing party of 70 Englishmen was warmly welcomed by the Natives, who generously supplied them with food. In a gesture of goodwill, the English entertained the Natives on the captain's ship and engaged in trade, acquiring valuable Spanish goods that the Natives had in their possession. Days later, the Hugh Gallant reappeared, reuniting with the fleet between Santa Maria Island and the mainland.

The fleet then headed north towards Mocha Island, sighting it on March 24, 1587. By the end of the month, they had arrived at Quintero, having inadvertently bypassed their intended stop at Valparaiso. They anchored near Concepción, where they observed Spaniards on horseback keeping a distance. Cavendish ventured about eight miles inland, impressed by the fertility of the valley. However, a betrayal unfolded when Tomé Hernandez, sent to parley with locals, instead escaped and alerted the Spanish. Nearly 200 Spaniards ambushed the English while they were collecting water, resulting in a skirmish that saw the English lose seven men and another nine captured, although they managed to drive the Spaniards off, inflicting twenty-four casualties.

Despite these setbacks, Cavendish remained in Quintero Bay until April 5, then set sail for Arica, entering the tropic zone. On April 23, 1587, they captured a barque laden with wine, renaming it George in honor of Saint George's Day. The George was integrated into their squadron. The following morning, they captured a large Spanish ship and four barks off Arica. Despite Arica's prepared defenses and an exchange of fire with Spanish shore batteries, Cavendish decided against storming the town. Instead, three ships in the harbor were set ablaze. The loot from this encounter included barrels of Chilean wine, various dispatches, and a Greek pilot named Jorge Carandino of Chios. Cavendish resorted to torturing prisoners to learn about the contents of letters they had discarded overboard.

By May 14, 1587, Cavendish reached Pisco, intercepting two Spanish merchant ships three days later. These ships were pillaged and burned. Using Pisco as a base, the English ships dispersed for independent actions. The Hugh Gallant captured a 300-ton vessel carrying timber from Guayaquil but had to abandon it as it was taking on water. Four days later, the Hugh Gallant took over Paita, capturing a bark in the harbor. Sixty men landed and occupied the town, its 300 inhabitants fleeing inland. When the inhabitants refused to pay a ransom, the English set fire to their homes before sailing north, taking with them some twenty-five pounds in silver pesos.

Upon their reunion, Cavendish and his fleet anchored off Puná Island on May 25, 1587, with the intention of careening and repairing their ships. The crew was initially captivated by the island's idyllic nature, abundant with fruit.

However, their tranquility was short-lived. While on land, about sixteen of Cavendish's men were ambushed by a large force of Spaniards and Indians from Quito, led by Captain Juan de Galarza. The initial skirmish scattered the English, but Cavendish quickly regained control by landing additional men, ultimately repelling the Spanish forces, albeit with the loss of nine sailors and three captured.

In retaliation, Cavendish ordered a destructive sweep of the island. Approximately 300 buildings were torched, a 250-ton ship was burned at anchor, and four more ships under construction were looted and set aflame. Even the church was not spared, with its bells being plundered. The English meticulously ensured that they left little of value behind on Puná Island before setting sail.

While near Guayaquil on June 5, 1587, the difficult decision was made to abandon the Hugh Gallant and the George due to a shortage of crew and the impracticality of repairs. Both vessels were stripped of valuable materials before being set alight, and the fleet departed eleven days later, steering a northerly course.

News of Cavendish's raids had reached Panama by early July, prompting the dispatch of two ships to intercept the English raiders. However, these efforts were belated. Similarly, Álvaro Manrique de Zúñiga, the Viceroy of New Spain, received news too late to take effective action.

On July 9, 1587, Cavendish captured a vessel. Although it carried no cargo, one of the captured pilots, Michael Sancius, divulged crucial information about an expected Manila galleon, which usually stopped at Cabo San Lucas on the Baja California peninsula before proceeding to Acapulco. This intelligence was further corroborated when another vessel was seized, which had been tasked with warning the galleon of the English presence.

Two weeks later, Cavendish's fleet entered the Copalita River, several leagues from Huatulco. A night operation using a pinnace and thirty men led to the capture of a bark from Sonsonate, laden with cacao and indigo. On August 2, 1587, Cavendish himself arrived at Huatulco, seizing and looting everything within a seven-mile radius over the course of a week. These raids proved to be lucrative. Before departing, Cavendish set the buildings and a merchant vessel in the harbor ablaze, continuing his journey northward.

Continuing his maritime exploits, Cavendish and his crew made landfall at Barra de Navidad on August 24, 1587. There, they swiftly detained the Spanish lookout and proceeded to destroy two 200-ton ships nearing completion under the direction of Antonio del Castillo and Juan Toscano. Additionally, they intercepted a messenger bearing the viceroy's warning about their presence. Before departing, they set fire to various buildings at the lagoon's entrance, leaving a trail of destruction in their wake.

On September 5, 1587, Cavendish's fleet sailed to the deserted bays of Santiago and Salagua near Manzanillo. They spent a week there, replenishing their water and provisions. The crew indulged in leisure activities, including swimming and pearl diving. Moving up the coast, they anchored at Tenacatitia Bay. Cavendish led thirty men inland to the village of Acatlan, where they burned most of the houses and defaced the church in a display of dominance and intimidation.

Leaving Tenacatitia Bay on September 14, Cavendish's next stop was Chacala, a sheltered bay. Although they found little of value, they captured two prisoners. Using them as leverage, Cavendish coerced the locals into providing fresh fruits, bread, and other food, which they loaded onto their ships before releasing the hostages and continuing their journey.

After departing Chacala on September 20, 1587, the fleet sailed past Compostela and anchored at the Tres Marias Islands for five days, where they caught iguanas and birds for sustenance. On October 4, in need of repairs, they anchored in the port of Mazatlán to careen their ships and adjust their cargo distribution. Cavendish then set course for the southwestern tip of Baja California, spending over a month at a location he named 'Aguada Segura', likely modern-day San Lucas Bay or San José del Cabo. Here, Cavendish prepared to intercept the Manila galleon.

The Manila galleons, limited by the Spanish Monarch to one or two ships per year, were laden with a year's worth of accumulated goods from the Spanish Philippines. These included silver from the mints in the Americas, traded for spices, silk, gold, and other valuable items from China and elsewhere. In 1587, there were two such galleons, the San Francisco and the Santa Ana. Both encountered a typhoon after departing the Philippines and were wrecked off the coast of Japan. Only the Santa Ana was salvageable, and after undergoing repairs, it resumed its voyage. Cavendish's strategic positioning to intercept the galleon was a calculated move, aiming to capitalize on the rich cargo these vessels were known to carry.

On the early morning of November 4, 1587, a lookout from Cavendish's crew sighted the 600-ton galleon Santa Ana, manned by over 200 men, off Cabo San Lucas. The English ships, after a lengthy pursuit, managed to catch up to the Santa Ana, which fortuitously lacked cannons, having been loaded with extra cargo instead. A fierce battle ensued, with Cavendish's ships firing cannonballs and grape shot at the galleon, while the Spanish crew attempted to retaliate with small arms. The Santa Ana sustained significant damage, including several holes below the waterline.

As the galleon began to sink, its captain, Tomás de Alzola, initially refused to surrender. However, the pilot, Alonso de Valladolid, persuaded him to negotiate for the lives of his crew in exchange for the cargo. With no other option, de Alzola surrendered. The English suffered minimal casualties, with two fatalities and ten wounded, compared to the Spanish losses of twelve killed and fifty wounded. The English then grappled the galleon, towing it into Aguada Segura, and lashed the ships together to consolidate their prize.

Given the vast difference in size between the English vessels, Content and Desire, and the Santa Ana, the English selectively transferred the rich cargo from the larger galleon. Among the one hundred and ninety captured Spaniards and Filipinos were notable figures like Sebastián Vizcaíno and Juan de Fuca. Cavendish also retained two Japanese sailors, Christopher and Cosmas, three boys from Manila, and a Portuguese traveler, Nicholas Roderigo, familiar with China, along with the defected pilot Alonso de Valladolid.

The English loaded all the gold, approximately 100 troy pounds (worth about 122,000 pesos), and selected the finest of the silks, damasks, musks, spices, wines, and ship's supplies. The total value of the cargo was estimated at about 2,100,000 pesos. After allowing the sailors to help themselves to the cargo, the less valuable items were discarded overboard. The Spanish crew were released with fresh provisions, water, wine, and even weapons for self-defense against native attacks.

On November 17, 1587, coinciding with Queen's Day, the English celebrated their victory with an extravagant feast of wine and food, culminating in a spectacular display of fireworks and the ceremonial burning of the Santa Ana, which was set adrift ablaze.

The following day, Desire and Content continued their voyage north. After the fire on the Santa Ana had extinguished, the Spanish survivors managed to construct a raft from the remains and signal for help. They were eventually rescued near Colima and taken to Acapulco on December 7, where they relayed the tale of their capture.

In October, while in the Gulf of California, Cavendish and his two ships, the Desire and Content, docked at an island above Mazatlan for ship careening. This maintenance was completed by November 17, 1587, at which point they embarked on their journey across the Pacific Ocean. However, during the night, the Content became separated from the Desire. Cavendish assumed the Content had returned to England, but the ship and its crew were never seen or heard from again, last observed heading north.

Cavendish, aboard the Desire, achieved a swift crossing of the Pacific, reaching the island of Guam on January 3, 1588. There, he traded iron tools with the natives in exchange for fresh supplies, water, and wood, before continuing his westward journey.

The Desire then sailed past the Mariana Islands, en route to the Spanish Philippines. On January 14, 1588, Cavendish navigated through the narrow San Bernardino Strait into the Sibuyan Sea, eventually reaching Panay. Approaching Manila, the English realized they lacked the strength to assault the capital. The Portuguese pilot Roderigo on board accused the Spanish pilot Tome de Alzola of plotting with local allies in Manila to attack them. A letter confirming this was discovered, and under torture, Alzola confessed. He was executed by hanging from the yardarm the following morning.

The Desire, laden with valuable cargo, made Cavendish cautious about engaging other vessels. However, he did conduct a raid on a large villa owned by Bishop Domingo de Salazar, looting its contents. An attempt to surprise attack a galleon under construction at the Areval shipyard was aborted when the landing party was detected early; they returned to the Desire without any casualties.

Despite these challenges, Cavendish gathered significant intelligence about Japan and the Chinese coast, information he hoped to utilize in future expeditions. He also acquired a large map of China, adding to his growing collection of valuable navigational and geographical knowledge.

Cavendish, now intent on returning to England, navigated the Desire away from the Philippines, passing the Moluccas and Bali, and arrived at the island of Lombok on March 1, 1588. Five days later, he anchored at Palabuhanratu Bay on the western end of Java. Initially, the reception from the natives was cold, but it soon warmed up thanks to a Negro sailor from the Santa Ana who spoke a dialect of Arabic understandable to the locals. Through his communication, the English managed to procure food and water during their four-day stay. The chief of the natives was even entertained on board the Desire, enjoying music played by the English crew.

The arrival of the English in Java also drew the attention of two Portuguese from a nearby factory. They came aboard the Desire, curious and concerned about the fate of their king, António, Prior of Crato. They had been informed by the Spanish that their king was dead, but Cavendish reassured them that King António was very much alive and in England, a revelation that brought them great joy. The Portuguese provided detailed insights into the regional politics and the riches of Java, and the natives promised a warm reception should the English return.

On March 16, 1588, Cavendish bid farewell to the natives and Portuguese of Java and set sail westward across the Indian Ocean. The voyage proceeded smoothly until May 10, when a storm hit, followed by a period of calm. On May 14, through the mist, they reached False Bay off Southern Africa, which Cavendish mistakenly thought was the Cape of Good Hope. There, they replenished their water and gathered fruit.

Continuing northward into the Atlantic, the Desire made a stop at the island of Saint Helena on June 8. Cavendish became one of the first Englishmen known to visit the island, which was claimed by the Portuguese, though none were encountered at the time. The ship was careened, and they restocked with turkeys, partridges, goats, and wild hogs found on the island. Cavendish spent two weeks exploring Saint Helena, taking detailed notes on its steep valleys and abundant fruit trees, further enriching his knowledge and experience as an explorer.

As August drew to a close, Cavendish and his crew aboard the Desire navigated past the Azores. On September 3, 1588, they encountered a Flemish hulk from

Lisbon, which brought them the momentous news of the Spanish Armada's defeat. This news was met with great jubilation among the English sailors.

Entering the English Channel in early September, the Desire was soon caught in a storm that severely damaged its sails. This storm was the same one that had battered the Spanish Armada, which was at that time retreating towards Santander. Despite the challenging weather conditions, Cavendish and his crew persevered.

On September 9, 1588, the Desire triumphantly sailed into Plymouth Harbor, welcomed by the exuberant cheers of the local populace. The return of Cavendish and his men marked the successful completion of their long and eventful journey, which had taken them across the globe. The crew's safe arrival back in England, especially after navigating through the aftermath of the storm that had devastated the Spanish Armada, was a cause for widespread celebration and marked a significant moment in the era of English maritime exploration.

In August 1591, Cavendish embarked on his second expedition, this time with the renowned navigator John Davis. Their journey took them further south than before, reaching the Strait of Magellan, before turning back to Brazil. In Brazil, they sought refuge and replenishment in Ilhabela, using it as a base to raid the towns of Santos and São Vicente.

As they ventured further north, they encountered fierce resistance from the Portuguese in the village of Vitória, which is now the capital of the State of Espirito Santo. This encounter resulted in the loss of most of their crew. One sailor who was left behind, Anthony Knivet, later recounted his experiences in Brazil.

With a significantly reduced crew, Cavendish then set sail across the Atlantic towards Saint Helena. Tragically, Cavendish never completed this journey, as he died under mysterious circumstances at the young age of 31, possibly near

Ascension Island in the South Atlantic in 1592. In his last letter, written just days before his death, Cavendish expressed his disillusionment and frustration, accusing John Davis of being a "villain" responsible for the failure of their mission.

Despite Cavendish's untimely death, John Davis persevered with the remaining crew and ships. He went on to discover the Falkland Islands before making the long journey back to England. The return was fraught with hardship, and many of the crew succumbed to starvation and illness. This second expedition, marked by both discovery and tragedy, added a complex chapter to the history of English exploration during this era.

Walter Raleigh

Sir Walter Raleigh, a figure shrouded in the mysteries of history, is thought to have been born on January 22, 1552 (or possibly 1554). His early years were spent at Hayes Barton, a house in the pastoral East Devon. As the youngest of Walter Raleigh Sr.'s five sons, he hailed from a family rooted in the junior branch of the Raleighs, historic 11th-century lords from North Devon. Despite sharing a lineage, these two branches displayed distinctly different heraldic symbols from the early days of heraldry around 1200.

Raleigh's mother, Katherine Champernowne, was a remarkable woman in her own right. She was the fourth daughter of Sir Philip Champernowne and Catherine Carew and had previously been married to Otes Gilbert. Her lineage linked Raleigh to the influential Champernowne family, connecting him to figures like Kat Ashley, Queen Elizabeth I's governess, and Sir Arthur Champernowne, a notable MP and Sheriff of Devon.

Raleigh's immediate family was a blend of full and half-siblings, including Carew Raleigh and the Gilbert brothers: John, Humphrey, and Adrian. Their association with the Champernowne family propelled them into prominence during the reigns of Elizabeth I and James I.

Living through the tumultuous reign of the Catholic Queen Mary I, Raleigh's Protestant family faced perilous times, with his father narrowly escaping execution. These experiences ingrained in Raleigh a deep aversion to

Catholicism, a sentiment he openly expressed after Elizabeth I ascended to the throne in 1558.

In 1569, Raleigh's adventurous spirit took him to France to aid the Huguenots in their religious civil wars. He enrolled at Oriel College, Oxford, in 1572 but left without a degree in 1574, later completing his education at the Inns of Court. Despite never formally studying law, Raleigh's experiences during these years, including witnessing the Battle of Moncontour, were significant.

Raleigh's quest for adventure continued with voyages in 1577 and 1579 alongside his half-brother Sir Humphrey Gilbert, seeking the elusive Northwest Passage. While they didn't find the passage, they did engage in successful raids on Spanish ships, adding to Raleigh's growing legend.

Between 1579 and 1580, Sir Walter Raleigh played a significant role in quelling the Desmond Rebellions. He was notably present at the siege of Smerwick, where he led a decisive operation that resulted in the beheading of around 600 Spanish and Italian soldiers. This event marked a critical moment in Raleigh's military career, showcasing his leadership and tactical acumen.

In September 1584, Queen Elizabeth I initiated a strategic move to colonize Ireland. She ordered a survey of the land, planning to divide and allocate it to her appointed "Undertakers," individuals tasked with overseeing the colonization efforts. This initiative was a key part of England's expansionist policies during the Elizabethan era.

In 1585, he was granted a substantial 40,000 acres (approximately 0.2% of Ireland) in the Munster Plantation. This land included the coastal town of Youghal and the village of Lismore, further up the Blackwater River. These acquisitions marked the beginning of Raleigh's tenure as a prominent Irish landlord.

Raleigh often resided in Youghal, making it his occasional home over his 17 years as an Irish landlord. He also spent time at Killua Castle in Clonmellon, County Westmeath. His influence in the region was notable, serving as the mayor of Youghal from 1588 to 1589. Raleigh's time in Ireland was also marked by his efforts to bring veterans of the earlier Roanoke Colony attempts to settle in Ireland. Notable among them were Thomas Hariot and John White, the latter having been the governor of the ill-fated 1587 Roanoke voyage.

He is credited with introducing potatoes to England and Ireland, a crop that would later become a staple in Irish agriculture and culture. The significance of this introduction cannot be overstated, as potatoes would become a central element of the Irish diet. Tragically, a potato failure in the 1800s would lead to the catastrophic Great Famine, highlighting the profound impact of Raleigh's introduction of the crop centuries earlier.

His circle in Munster included other notable English figures, such as the poet Edmund Spenser, who had also been granted land in the Irish colonies. However, Raleigh's management of his Irish estates encountered various challenges, contributing to a decline in his fortunes. By 1602, these difficulties led him to sell his lands to Richard Boyle, the 1st Earl of Cork. Boyle would go on to prosper under the reigns of kings James I and Charles I, in stark contrast to the waning fortunes of Raleigh.

On March 25, 1584, Queen Elizabeth I bestowed upon the daring Sir Walter Raleigh a royal charter, a passport to adventure and discovery. This charter wasn't just a document; it was a ticket to explore and claim uncharted lands, to seek out riches in territories not yet touched by Christian rulers. The deal was enticing: Raleigh could keep a fifth of any gold and silver unearthed. Time, however, was of the essence, as he had only seven years to establish a settlement, or the opportunity would vanish like a ship into the horizon.

The story takes a dramatic turn with the launch of the Philip Amadas and Arthur Barlowe expedition on April 27, 1584. Their mission: to scout the vast expanses of North America and unlock its secrets. Their return in August 1584 was not just with tales of a new land, but with two native inhabitants, Manteo and Wanchese. Their accounts painted a vivid picture of this new world, aptly named "Virginia" in honor of the Virgin Queen, Elizabeth I.

In 1585 Raleigh, driven by dreams of wealth and a strategic base for privateering against Spain, sends a militarized group to North America. Led by the valiant Sir Richard Grenville and governed by Ralph Lane, they establish a colony on Roanoke Island, poised to be the first English settlement in the New World. Yet, this venture teeters on the edge of disaster. Clashes with local inhabitants, a dire food shortage, and failed resupply attempts lead to a desperate departure with Sir Francis Drake in June 1586. The twist? Sir Richard Grenvile arrives just after the Lane colony's departure, leaving supplies and 15 men behind on Roanoke Island – men who would vanish into the annals of history, their fate a lingering mystery.

Sir Walter Raleigh orchestrated a second expedition on July 22, 1587, setting his sights once more on Roanoke Island. This time, the cast of characters was more varied, with whole families joining the adventure, all under the leadership of John White. Shortly after their arrival in America, White embarked on a return voyage to England, intending to resupply the colony within a year. But fate had other plans.

The first twist in their tale came when Queen Elizabeth I, amidst the looming threat of the Spanish Armada, commandeered all ships for defense, including those meant for Roanoke. It wasn't until after England triumphed over Spain in 1588 that the vessels were freed for their original purpose.

When White's fleet, now finally en route to Roanoke, is lured off course. Enticed by tales of Spanish treasures in Cuba, as spun by an experienced Portuguese navigator hired by Raleigh, the crew veered towards the Caribbean. White's concerns about the delay were overshadowed by visions of untold riches.

Upon their belated arrival at Roanoke, three years behind schedule, they were greeted not by the settlers but by an eerie silence. The cryptic message "CROATOAN" and the letters "CRO" etched into tree trunks were the only breadcrumbs left behind. White had previously agreed with the settlers that they would leave such a marker if they relocated, hinting they might have sought refuge on Croatoan Island. However, a brewing hurricane thwarted any attempt to follow this lead, shrouding their fate in mystery. They could have succumbed to starvation, been lost at sea, or swept away by the storm of 1588. The "Lost Colony," as it came to be known, faded into legend, its secrets untold.

Meanwhile, Raleigh, the architect of these ventures, never set foot in North America. His later expeditions in 1595 and 1617 took him to South America's Orinoco river basin, chasing the elusive El Dorado. Despite the substantial investments from Raleigh and his friends, these quests failed to yield the continuous revenue necessary to sustain an American colony.

In 1580, Sir Walter Raleigh embarked on a daring venture, joining the fray in Ireland to quell the 2nd Desmond Rebellion. By December 1581, his heroics on the battlefield brought him back to England, where he quickly became a favorite at Queen Elizabeth I's court. His support for the Protestant Church in Ireland had caught the Queen's eye, earning him favor and recognition.

Raleigh's star continued to rise, and in 1585, he was knighted, a testament to his growing influence and prestige. His responsibilities expanded dramatically: he was made warden of the stannaries, overseeing the tin mines of Cornwall and Devon, appointed Lord Lieutenant of Cornwall, and even became the vice-admiral of the two counties. His political influence also grew as he served as a member of parliament for Devonshire in 1585 and 1586. During this period, he also received the monumental right to colonize America.

Raleigh's ventures extended to the seas when he commissioned shipbuilder R. Chapman of Deptford to construct a vessel for him. Initially named Ark, the ship was renamed Ark Raleigh, following the custom of naming ships after their owners. In a twist of fate, Queen Elizabeth I bought the ship from Raleigh in January 1587 for a staggering sum, which effectively cleared a debt Raleigh owed to the crown. Henceforth, the ship was known as Ark Royal.

The year 1586 brought another intriguing episode when Raleigh's men captured the Spanish explorer Pedro Sarmiento de Gamboa. Raleigh, engaging in a game of espionage and diplomacy, held Gamboa in his house, engaging in extensive conversations and passing messages to the Spanish ambassador, which eventually reached King Philip II of Spain. Raleigh even contemplated defecting to Spain and selling the Ark, but Philip, while declining to buy the ship, encouraged the exchange of information.

In 1588, amidst the looming threat of the Spanish Armada, Raleigh played a role in the defenses at Devon. Remarkably, the Ark Royal, the ship he once offered to Spain and later sold to the crown, served as the flagship of Lord High Admiral Howard in this pivotal moment in history.

In 1592, Sir Walter Raleigh found himself showered with royal favors by Queen Elizabeth I. Among these were the grand Durham House in the Strand and the picturesque Sherborne estate in Dorset. He also assumed the prestigious role of Captain of the Yeomen of the Guard. Despite these honors, Raleigh had not ascended to the highest echelons of state office.

The previous year, 1591, marked a personal turning point for Raleigh when he secretly wed Elizabeth "Bess" Throckmorton, a younger lady-in-waiting to the Queen, who was pregnant at the time. The couple welcomed a son, believed to be named Damerei, who tragically succumbed to plague in October 1592. Bess briefly returned to her court duties, but their clandestine marriage was eventually uncovered. The revelation led to Raleigh's imprisonment and Bess's dismissal from court, both confined in the Tower of London in June 1592.

Raleigh's incarceration was briefly interrupted in August 1592, when he was released to oversee an expedition against the Spanish. This venture led to the capture of the Madre de Deus, a merchant ship laden with riches, off Flores. Raleigh's role in dividing the spoils landed him back in the Tower, but by early 1593, he was free and serving as a member of Parliament.

Raleigh's return to the Queen's favor took several years, during which he traveled extensively. Despite their trials, he and Bess remained deeply committed to each other, welcoming two more sons, Walter in 1593 and Carew in 1605.

In his political life, Raleigh was elected as a burgess of Mitchell, Cornwall, in the 1593 parliament. He retired to his Sherborne estate, where he built Sherborne Lodge (now known as Sherborne New Castle), completed in 1594. There, he fostered friendships with local gentry like Sir Ralph Horsey and Charles Thynne. However, his time was not without controversy; a heated debate about religion with Reverend Ralph Ironsides at a dinner party sparked unfounded charges of atheism against Raleigh, though these were eventually dismissed. In Parliament, he continued to voice his opinions on religious and naval matters.

In a daring voyage, Sir Walter Raleigh set sail from Plymouth on February 6, 1595, charting a course toward the Azores for essential supplies before crossing the Atlantic. En route, near the Canary Islands, Raleigh's crew captured a Spanish ship off Tenerife, seizing a substantial cache of firearms from its cargo. The very next day, they commandeered a Flemish vessel, acquiring 20 hogsheads of Spanish wine.

Upon reaching the Caribbean in late March, Raleigh found himself isolated, having lost contact with two allied expeditions during the transatlantic journey. The first, led by Dudley and Popham, had departed the rendezvous area around February 9 after capturing several Spanish ships and deciding to return to England with their prizes. Simultaneously, the Preston Somers

Expedition, intended to divert Spanish attention from Raleigh, had ventured further west, missing their planned meeting. Unfazed, they continued their raid, successfully assaulting La Guaira, Coro, and even daringly taking Caracas after navigating through mountain passes.

Raleigh's primary goal was the Spanish colony of Trinidad, specifically targeting San José de Oruña, established by Berrio in 1592. Landing on the southern part of the island, he discovered the locals cultivating high-quality tobacco and sugar cane. Sailing across the Gulf of Paria, he was drawn to shore at Terra de Brea by the smell of tar. Guided by the Caribs to a pitch lake (the world's largest natural asphalt lake), Raleigh recognized its value for ship caulking and took several barrels, inadvertently "discovering" the lake.

On April 4, Raleigh and a hundred soldiers took the small stockade at Puerto de España, overpowering the modest Spanish garrison and advancing inland towards San José de Oruña. Achieving the element of surprise, they launched a swift nighttime assault that lasted barely an hour, overpowering the nearly fifty-strong garrison. The Spanish general Mayor Alvaro Jorge was captured, but the more significant prize was Governor de Berrio, who pleaded for the town's mercy. Raleigh agreed, planning to use it as a base for exploring the Orinoco River. He also freed five native Indian chiefs whom Berrio had cruelly chained, tortured, and left to starve.

A fort was constructed in anticipation of any Spanish retaliation, and Raleigh began his quest for the fabled city of El Dorado. Interrogating de Berrio, Raleigh learned about Manoa and El Dorado, but despite de Berrio's attempts to dissuade him, Raleigh was undeterred in his pursuit of the legendary city.

On April 15, 1595, Sir Walter Raleigh embarked on a daring journey from his base in the modified Gallego, designed for river navigation, with a hundred men and two wherries. They were racing against time, spurred by rumors of a looming Spanish expedition to the area. Indeed, the rumors were true; Captain Felipe de Santiago, a trusted officer of Berrio, was trailing Raleigh's expedition from Margarita Island with a number of canoes.

Navigating the complex waters of the Orinoco river basin, Raleigh's crew faced challenges with shallow waters, necessitating further modifications to the Gallego and the construction of rafts to lighten the load. As they delved deeper, the dense jungle and a maze of waterways tested their resolve, and they even lost an Indian guide named Ferdinando under mysterious circumstances.

Despite these setbacks, Raleigh's party soon found an Indian village where they secured not only a new guide but also vital supplies of fish, bread, and fowl. The journey continued, leading them to the expansive savannas of the Orinoco valley. Tragically, during this leg, a crew member was attacked and killed by a crocodile, a harrowing event that prompted Raleigh to caution his men against the dangers lurking in the river.

On April 27, the Spanish, led by Santiago and still in pursuit, saw an opportunity to ambush the English when their rear became separated. However, their surprise attack backfired as they found themselves trapped in a narrow river bend. The English, led by Gifford, quickly turned the tables, launching a counterattack that overpowered the Spanish. The English suffered no losses, while the Spanish sustained casualties and were forced to retreat into the woods, leaving their canoes as prizes for Raleigh's men.

Santiago, demoralized by this defeat, withdrew to Margarita Island. Raleigh's team, now bolstered by the captured canoes filled with food, supplies, and tools for ore detection, continued their expedition with renewed vigor, guided by one of the three Indians they had captured, who had mistaken them for Spaniards and pleaded for mercy.

A day after their victorious encounter with the Spanish, Sir Walter Raleigh's expedition reached a significant junction of rivers, identifying it as the Caroni River. Here, they first met the Warao and then the Pemons, two indigenous Amerindian groups. By displaying a Spanish canoe they had captured, Raleigh's crew quickly established peaceful relations with these tribes.

In a large village, likely near what is now Ciudad Guayana, they encountered an elderly chieftain named Topiawari. Raleigh endeared himself to Topiawari by declaring his opposition to the Spanish, who were deeply unpopular among the natives. Topiawari shared tales of a rich culture in the mountains, which Raleigh eagerly interpreted as a potential connection to the wealthy Inca civilization of Peru, possibly even the mythical city of Manoa. Forming an alliance against the Spanish, Raleigh left two men as hostages, taking Topiawari's son as a guide.

Raleigh and his lieutenant, Kemys, ventured further up the Caroni River with Topiawari's son, scouting for gold and mines, and continuously forging alliances with local tribes. They collected rocks, hoping they contained gold.

The expedition soon encountered a dramatic change in the landscape, including a tepuy (tabletop mountain). Raleigh marveled at Mount Roraima's vast summit and steep cliffs, and was awestruck by the numerous waterfalls, one towering higher than any church spire he had seen. This part of the journey led Raleigh to describe the surroundings as the most beautiful he had ever seen. There were speculative claims that Raleigh might have been the first European to see Angel Falls, but these are generally considered unlikely.

After traveling nearly 400 miles inland and with the onset of the rainy season, Raleigh decided to turn back. They returned to Topiawari's village, where his son agreed to accompany Raleigh to England and was christened Gualtero. Raleigh then learned of a gold mine near Mount Iconuri and dispatched Lawrence Keymis to investigate. Though Keymis didn't find the mine, he collected quartz rocks that indicated potential value.

Upon returning to San Jose, Raleigh's crew, remarkably healthy thanks to the native diet, looted and burned the fort despite de Berrío's protests. Raleigh then raided Margarita Island for supplies and sacked Cumaná and Riohacha, releasing de Berrío without a ransom.

On July 13, Raleigh reunited with Preston and Somers, learning of their conquests in Caracas, La Guaira, and Coro. Adverse winds scrapped plans to seek out the Roanoke colony, and the expedition returned to England by the end of August 1595, marking the end of a remarkable yet arduous journey.

In 1596, Sir Walter Raleigh's adventurous spirit led him to participate in the pivotal capture of Cádiz, an engagement during which he sustained an injury. His naval prowess was further showcased in 1597 as the rear admiral of the Islands Voyage to the Azores, a principal command reflecting his esteemed position. Upon his return, Raleigh played a crucial role in defending England against the 3rd Spanish Armada in the autumn of 1597. The Armada, initially a formidable threat in the Channel, was ultimately scattered and devastated by a storm off Ireland. Alongside Lord Howard of Effingham, Raleigh organized a fleet that successfully intercepted a Spanish ship, retrieving vital intelligence about Spanish plans.

Raleigh's political influence continued to grow as he was elected to parliament for Dorset in 1597 and for Cornwall in 1601, a unique accomplishment in the Elizabethan era for representing three different counties.

As the governor of Jersey from 1600 to 1603, Raleigh significantly upgraded the island's defenses. This included constructing the Fort Isabella Bellissima, or Elizabeth Castle, bolstering the protection of Saint Helier.

Though Raleigh had regained Queen Elizabeth's favor, her death on March 24, 1603, marked a downturn in his fortunes. He was arrested on July 19, 1603, at the Old Exeter Inn in Ashburton, accused of treason in the Main Plot against Elizabeth's successor, James I, and was subsequently imprisoned in the Tower of London.

Raleigh's trial, which began on November 17 at Winchester Castle's Great Hall, was notable for his self-representation. The primary evidence against him was the confession of his friend, Henry Brooke, Lord Cobham. Raleigh fiercely demanded Cobham's testimony, arguing for the right to face his accuser, a stance that later influenced the development of the common law right to confront one's accusers. Despite his efforts, Raleigh was convicted, though King James I ultimately spared his life.

During his lengthy imprisonment in the Tower, Raleigh authored the ambitious but incomplete "The Historie of the World." This work, drawing on a multitude of sources in six languages, focused not on England but on the ancient world, with a particular emphasis on geography. Despite intending to provide counsel to King James I, the King criticized the work for being overly critical of monarchs. Raleigh remained in the Tower until 1616, during which time his son Carew was conceived and born.

In 1617, Sir Walter Raleigh, having been pardoned by King James I, embarked on a second quest to Venezuela in pursuit of the legendary El Dorado. This expedition, however, spiraled into tragedy. Defying both Raleigh's explicit orders and peace treaties with Spain, a group of his men led by his close associate, Lawrence Kemys, attacked the Spanish outpost of Santo Tomé de Guayana on the Orinoco River. During this assault, Raleigh's son Walter was tragically killed. Kemys, overwhelmed with guilt and facing Raleigh's refusal to forgive him, took his own life.

Upon Raleigh's return to England, the Spanish ambassador, Count Gondomar, was incensed by the breach of peace and insisted on the reinstatement of Raleigh's previously commuted death sentence. King James, under diplomatic pressure, complied. Raleigh, escorted back to London by Sir Lewis Stukley, missed several chances to escape.

Raleigh met his end on October 29, 1618, in the Old Palace Yard at the Palace of Westminster. Facing execution with remarkable composure, he told the executioner, "Let us dispatch, at this hour my ague comes upon me. I would not have my enemies think I quaked from fear." Upon inspecting the executioner's axe, he commented, "This is a sharp Medicine, but it is a Physician for all diseases and miseries." His final words, urging the hesitant executioner to action, were, "What dost thou fear? Strike, man, strike!"

Raleigh's contributions to English culture included popularizing tobacco smoking, introduced to him possibly by Thomas Hariot. A poignant reminder of his habit was found after his execution – a tobacco pouch with the Latin inscription "Comes meus fuit in illo miserrimo tempore" ("It was my companion at that most miserable time").

After his beheading, Raleigh's head was embalmed and given to his wife, while his body was initially intended for burial in Beddington, Surrey, Lady Raleigh's home. Ultimately, he was laid to rest in St. Margaret's, Westminster. Lady Raleigh poignantly remarked, "The Lords have given me his dead body, though they have denied me his life. God hold me in my wits." Legend has it that she kept his head in a velvet bag until her death, after which it was interred with his body in St. Margaret's Church.

Though Raleigh's reputation had diminished since his Elizabethan prime, his execution was widely viewed as both unnecessary and unjust, a sentiment echoed by one of the judges at his trial: "The justice of England has never been so degraded and injured as by the condemnation of the honourable Sir Walter Raleigh."

John Ward

Born around 1553 into a family struggling with poverty in Kent, England, the early years of this individual were marked by a humble existence, primarily engaged in fishing the tidal waters of his coastal homeland. His life, however, was far from exemplary. Known as an inveterate wastrel, he was frequently consumed by drunkenness and exhibited a morose disposition. Often seen sitting in sullen silence, he would speak with a sharp tongue and display a bitter envy towards the prosperity of others.

A pivotal moment in his life coincided with the historic defeat of the Spanish Armada. Like many mariners of his era, he found an opportunity in privateering—a quasi-legal form of piracy sanctioned by Queen Elizabeth I. The Queen granted licenses to those who wished to raid and plunder Spanish ships, a reflection of the deep-seated animosity towards Spain at the time.

The arrangement with the Crown was straightforward: the Queen's coffers would receive a modest five percent of the spoils, while agents of the Lord Admiral claimed a heftier ten percent. The remainder was split between the ship's owner and its crew. Little is known about his effectiveness as a privateer during these formative years, as historical records from this period remain sparse. Yet, it was during these ventures that he honed the skills that would later define his notorious career in piracy.

The cessation of the Anglo-Spanish war in the summer of 1604, under the reign of James VI and I, successor to Elizabeth I, brought an abrupt end to his maritime endeavors. The new monarch outlawed all privateering activities, leaving him and many others in his profession jobless and adrift. An associate, Andrew Barker, recounted his lamentations over this drastic turn of events. He longingly reminisced about the days of unbridled freedom on the seas—days filled with reckless indulgence in song, drink, and debauchery, and where acts of violence were as commonplace as a baker swatting flies. He mourned the loss of what he perceived as a golden age, a time when the vast ocean was their realm to roam and plunder at will.

In Portsmouth, a pivotal rumor reached Ward, setting the stage for a dramatic shift in his life's trajectory. It was said that a modest merchant ship, moored in the harbor, contained the valuable possessions of a Catholic merchant preparing to relocate from England to France. Seizing this opportunity, Ward rallied a group of 30 seafaring associates to commandeer the ship and its supposed treasure. Under the cover of night, his motley crew executed a daring raid, swiftly overpowering the two unsuspecting watchmen on board and securing them in chains. Without delay, they navigated the commandeered vessel into the open waters of the English Channel, embarking on a fateful journey.

However, Ward's dreams of riches were soon dashed. The ship's owner, having anticipated such a plot, had prudently moved all his valuables ashore. Ward and his men found themselves in possession of a ship devoid of any treasure. Undeterred, they continued their voyage and soon encountered a French merchant ship off the Isles of Scilly. Ward, feigning friendship, engaged the French captain in hours of amicable conversation. But this ruse was short-lived; revealing his true intent, Ward unleashed his pirate battle cry. In a matter of seconds, his crew boarded the French vessel, swiftly taking control of both the ship and its crew. This marked Ward's first taste of success in his newfound career as a pirate.

Understanding the need for a larger crew to man a larger ship, Ward set course for Cawsand in Cornwall. There, he enticed a group of smugglers and fishermen with the promise of a once-in-a-lifetime adventure. He painted a picture of the Mediterranean's riches, with its traders, merchantmen, and galleons ripe for the taking. Ward and his expanded crew set sail, eyes set on the bountiful waters of the Mediterranean.

Their initial conquests were promising. The first was a coastal trader, heavily laden with goods. The second, a two-masted transport ship, was primarily used for transporting galley slaves. With these prizes in tow, Ward steered towards Algiers, a notorious haven for pirates. However, fortune was not on his side. Just months before his arrival, an English privateer named Richard Gifford had attacked the city. The governor of Algiers, harboring a newfound animosity towards Englishmen, was not inclined to welcome Ward or his crew.

Ward, undeterred by the hostility he faced in Algiers, set his sights on the bustling port of Salé, located on the Atlantic coast of Morocco. This haven was a notorious hotspot for seafaring outlaws and vagabonds. Its pirates, famed for their audacity, had been preying on merchant ships for years. Their daring had escalated to the point where they ventured to raid the shores of England and France, capturing entire villages to be sold in the sprawling slave markets of North Africa. Salé's reputation as a pirate stronghold was well-earned, and it promised Ward a welcoming environment for his endeavors.

Upon his arrival in Salé, Ward found himself among kindred spirits. The port was a melting pot of piracy, with English and Dutch pirates already established and thriving there. These seasoned sea robbers readily agreed to join forces with Ward, recognizing the value of his leadership and experience. Ward seized the opportunity to sell his recently acquired booty in this new, lawless market. He then dedicated his efforts to refitting and upgrading his ships, preparing for the next chapter of his piratical career.

His next destination was Tunis, a bustling port city with the allure of becoming his permanent base of operations. This decision would prove to be a defining moment in his life. Tunis, at the time, was under nominal rule by a pasha appointed by the Ottoman Sultan in distant Istanbul. However, the true power in Tunis during Ward's arrival in 1605 lay in the hands of Uthman Dey, the formidable leader of the janissary soldiers. The janissaries, known as the Sultan's elite household troops and bodyguards, were a force to be reckoned with.

Uthman Dey, a figure both cunning and ruthless, had masterminded the formation of a powerful guild of corsairs. These corsairs, under Uthman Dey's shrewd leadership, had turned the Mediterranean into their hunting ground, preying on shipping across its expanse. Ward's arrival in Tunis coincided with the zenith of Uthman Dey's power, presenting him with an opportunity to align with one of the most feared and respected figures in the Mediterranean's piratical circles.

Uthman Dey, despite his authority and influence in Tunis, faced a quandary when Ward and his ragtag crew of Cornish smugglers and roughnecks from England's West Country arrived at his doorstep. This motley band presented a stark contrast to the disciplined and immaculately uniformed janissaries who maintained order in the city. Ward's pirates were a sight to behold: many toothless, sporting unruly beards, and clad in an eccentric mix of stolen velvet doublets and silk waistcoats, they seemed like characters out of a seafarer's tall tale.

Yet, amidst this apparent disarray, Uthman Dey discerned potential. He recognized in Ward not just a daring pirate, but a master of his trade. Dey, ever the strategist, decided to allow Ward to establish Tunis as his base of operations. This agreement, however, came with a condition: Uthman Dey demanded a cut of the profits from Ward's ventures.

In the wake of this agreement, Ward embarked on a spree of maritime conquests. His captures were nothing short of spectacular. Among them was the English merchantman named John Baptist, laden with opulent damasks.

Displaying a flair for theatrics, Ward rechristened the ship the Little John, an homage to the legendary English folk hero. Another of his prizes, suggesting a hidden whimsical side to the otherwise dour pirate, was aptly renamed the Gift.

The spring of that inaugural year in Tunis saw Ward's fleet swell with numerous seized ships. One notable capture was the Rubin, a 300-ton behemoth brimming with pepper, indigo, and a trove of luxury goods sourced from Alexandria, destined for the markets of Venice. His haul also included the Elizabeth, Charity, and Pearl. Then there was the Trojan of London, whose English crew faced a grim fate: enslaved for the mere act of firing a single shot in self-defense.

Ward's exploits during this period marked a significant escalation in his piratical career, transforming him from a mere rogue of the seas into a formidable force in the Mediterranean. His success not only filled his coffers but also bolstered his reputation, drawing the attention of friend and foe alike across the sea-faring world.

Ward's alliance with Uthman Dey proved to be immensely beneficial, as evidenced by the grandiose gift he received: a substantial plot of land in Tunis. On this land, Ward embarked on an ambitious project to construct a mansion of such scale and opulence that it would have been beyond the wildest dreams of anyone in his humble English hometown. Visitors to this palatial residence were left in awe. One fellow Englishman, upon seeing the mansion, remarked that it was more befitting a prince than a pirate. The mansion was a testament to Ward's newfound wealth and status, adorned with rich marble and alabaster stones, its halls echoing with the whispers of luxury and power.

In this exotic setting, Ward began to adopt the lifestyle of an Oriental potentate, immersing himself in a life of extraordinary luxury and power. His transformation was not just in his opulent living conditions but also in his personal demeanor and appearance. He dressed in elaborate and expensive garments, his meals were lavish affairs prepared by two personal chefs, and his every whim was attended to by a retinue of devoted followers. He even had a personal taster, a luxury reserved for the highest nobility, to ensure his safety and the quality of his food.

In April of 1607, while cruising along the Turkish coast, Ward's fortune took yet another remarkable turn. From the deck of his ship, he sighted a colossal merchant vessel on the horizon. As they drew closer, the size of the ship became apparent, stunning Ward and his crew. The Reniera e Soderina was a massive argosy, estimated to be fourteen or fifteen hundred tons. She was a titan among ships, sailing from Aleppo and laden with an incredibly valuable cargo of silks, indigo, and cotton. Her massive size, however, was her downfall. The argosy was so heavily burdened that she struggled to maneuver in the light winds, rendering her an easy target for Ward's swifter, more agile vessels.

Ward, with his keen eye for opportunity, recognized the potential prize before him. Here was a chance to capture not just any ship, but a leviathan of the seas, brimming with treasures that would further cement his status as one of the most formidable pirates of his era. The pursuit of the Reniera e Soderina was not just a chase for wealth; it was a pursuit of glory, a testament to Ward's audacity and skill as a pirate of unparalleled renown.

The air was thick with anticipation as Ward, with a fierce determination in his eyes, bellowed his battle cry. The cannons roared to life, hurling cannonballs with deadly precision into the hull of the Reniera e Soderina. The projectiles tore through the timbers, puncturing the ship's sides five times and igniting bales of hay within. The Reniera e Soderina desperately returned fire, but her shots fell short, unable to land a single hit on Ward's agile vessels.

For three grueling hours, the bombardment continued, the sea echoing with the thunder of cannons and the cries of men. Ward's crew, sensing victory was near, readied themselves to board the beleaguered ship. In a final bid to rally his crew, the captain of the Reniera e Soderina offered them a choice: surrender or fight. The crew, stirred by a sense of duty and desperation, vowed to fight and armed themselves, gathering mostly on the quarterdeck, preparing for the inevitable clash.

Just as Ward's men were about to grapple the ship, a final, devastating volley was unleashed. Six rounds of lethal chain shot screamed through the air, shredding the Reniera e Soderina's rigging and sails, and wreaking havoc among her crew. Two men were instantly torn apart, their gruesome fate sending a wave of panic through their comrades, causing many to drop their weapons in horror.

In the midst of this chaos, Ward himself, embodying the very spirit of a pirate king, leaped aboard the Reniera e Soderina. His presence on the deck was like a force of nature, inspiring his men with a courage so fierce it seemed to defy death itself. The ensuing battle was brutal and relentless. Ward, with an unyielding resolve, fought at the forefront, pushing his men towards victory. "In the end, our captain had the sunshine: he boarded her, subdued her, chained her men like slaves," recounted one of his crew. With the ship and her crew finally under his control, Ward triumphantly sailed the Reniera e Soderina back to Tunis.

The capture of the Reniera e Soderina marked the pinnacle of Ward's career in piracy, a feat that he would never quite replicate. Following the ship's refitting in Tunis, he assembled a crew and set sail on her maiden voyage as a pirate vessel. Yet, fate had a cruel twist in store. The modifications Ward had made to the cannon deck compromised the ship's structural integrity. During a fierce storm, the once-mighty Reniera e Soderina, now weakened and battered, succumbed to the merciless sea, sinking with the tragic loss of 350 men. Ward, narrowly escaping the same fate, retreated to Tunis aboard one of his smaller ships, a somber shadow of the triumph he had so recently enjoyed.

The catastrophic sinking of the Reniera e Soderina cast a long, dark shadow over Ward's once-formidable reputation. The news of this disaster spread rapidly through Tunis, turning him into a figure of widespread resentment and scorn, especially among those who had lost family and friends. His situation became increasingly precarious, and he found himself heavily dependent on the protection of Uthman Dey, the only ally of consequence he had left.

By around 1610, faced with dwindling options and a tarnished reputation, Ward and his crew made a radical and historic decision: they chose to 'turn Turk', converting to Islam and resolving to make Tunis their permanent home. In this dramatic transformation, Ward adopted the name Yusuf Reis and even entered into a second marriage, despite having a wife back in England. Observers in his later years painted a picture of a man greatly diminished from his piratical heyday. Described as "very short with little hair, and that quite white, bald in front," he was a man who spoke infrequently, and when he did, it was often laced with curses. He was seen as a habitual drunkard, a man who had lost himself outside the realm of piracy, described as "a fool and an idiot out of his trade."

Yet, even as Ward's personal life spiraled downwards, his legend grew exponentially. He became the subject of numerous plays, pamphlets, ballads, and books. These works oscillated between vilifying and romanticizing his life as a corsair, capturing the public's imagination with tales of his exploits at sea.

One of the most renowned ballads about him was "Captain Ward and the Rainbow," which narrates a fictional encounter where the King of England sends the ship Royal Rainbow to capture the notorious pirate. In the ballad, Ward triumphs over the royal ship, and it concludes with a defiant proclamation to the King of England: "If he reign king of all the land, I will reign king at sea." These words became an enduring epitaph for a man who, for a significant part of his life, was perhaps England's most infamous pirate, ruling the seas with an iron hand.

Despite the infamy and myths surrounding him, Ward continued his raids on Mediterranean shipping, eventually commanding an entire fleet of corsairs. His flagship was a formidable sixty-gunner Venetian vessel. However, after 1612, Ward chose to retire from active piracy. Instead, he dedicated his later years to teaching younger corsairs the arts of gunnery and navigation, sharing the wealth of experience he had accumulated over his notorious career.

Ward lived out his final years in Tunis, enjoying the wealth he had amassed through his life of piracy. He lived in opulent comfort until his death in 1622 at the age of 70, possibly succumbing to the plague. His story, woven into the fabric of maritime folklore, left an indelible mark on the history of piracy, immortalizing him as a legendary figure whose life oscillated between glory, infamy, and tragedy.

Zheng Zhilong

Zheng Zhilong's life story is a fascinating journey through Chinese history, deeply rooted in the shifting tides of dynastic changes and social upheavals. Born in Fujian Province, he was the son of Zheng Shaozu, a dedicated mid-level financial official serving the local government, and Lady Huang, his mother. The Zheng family, like many other clans in Fujian, had a rich history that traced back to Northern China. However, the tumultuous events of the Uprising of the Five Barbarians and the Disaster of Yongjia during the Five Barbarians period forced them, along with many other northern refugees, to seek safety in the southeastern reaches of China.

Settling initially in Fujian, the Zheng family's journey was marked by several relocations, reflecting the unstable and dynamic nature of the times. They moved to Zhangzhou and later to Nan'an, adapting to new environments and challenges. Historical records from 1144 to 1210 indicate that Zheng Zhilong's ancestors, including Zheng Boke, embarked on a significant migration from Qiangtian to Longxi county, then to Nan'an. Zheng Boke, a notable figure in Zheng Zhilong's lineage, was instrumental in establishing the family's roots in this new land.

The Zheng family history is richly detailed in the "Selected Works of Genealogical Data of Fujian and Taiwan Relations." This compilation provides insights into the intricate movements of the family across various regions. The genealogy reveals that the Zheng family, upon arriving in Zhangzhou, settled in Longxi at the end of the Song dynasty, in what is now known as

Yangxi Village of Bangshan Town, Longhai. Their journey continued in the Yuan dynasty, moving from Yangxi to Lushan, now recognized as Fujian Longhai Yanyan in Zhengu County. The family's continuous relocation, from ancient county to Nan'an, underscores the adaptability and resilience that were characteristic of the Zheng clan.

An interesting footnote in Zheng Zhilong's family history is the epitaph of the 13th ancestor of the Anping Zheng of Jinjiang, penned by Hong Chengchou, a prominent governor of the Ming dynasty. Hong's writings offer a glimpse into the family's history, highlighting their migration to the Fengting Pavilion in Xianyou, a significant site in their ancestral journey. He mentions the Fengting Bridge, a landmark still associated with the Zheng family's legacy. The epitaph also sheds light on the family's forced southward movement to the Anping area of Jinjiang, present-day Anhai, due to frequent conflicts in the region.

Zheng Zhilong's family background, rich in historical movements and cultural shifts, paints a vivid picture of a family continually adapting to the changing landscapes of Chinese history.

The story of Zheng's childhood, as recounted in contemporary biographies, is a captivating tale that blurs the line between myth and reality, illustrating the early signs of his remarkable character. According to a possibly apocryphal yet enchanting narrative, young Zheng and his brothers, driven by a childlike yearning, set their hearts on tasting the sweet longan fruit. Their adventure began with a fruit tree that stood majestically in an enclosed courtyard, its branches generously overflowing with ripe fruits, tantalizingly hanging over the wall into the street.

In their innocent eagerness, the boys resorted to throwing stones, hoping to dislodge some of the fruit clusters. However, their mischievous plan inadvertently led to an unexpected twist. The courtyard, unbeknownst to them, belonged to the governor of Quanzhou City. As fate would have it, the governor himself was struck by the errant stones. This unforeseen incident quickly escalated, and the boys, realizing the gravity of their mischief, fled the scene. However, their escape was short-lived as they were soon apprehended and brought before the very governor they had inadvertently offended.

In a surprising turn of events, the governor, upon encountering young Zheng, was struck not by anger but by the boy's youthful charisma and apparent destiny. In a moment of magnanimity, the governor not only forgave Zheng but also prophetically declared, "This is the face of one destined for wealth and nobility." This incident, whether factual or embellished, encapsulates the essence of Zheng's character: a young boy, untamed and audacious, reaching for the proverbial low-hanging fruit, only to find himself in trouble but emerging unscathed and perhaps even favored by fortune.

The records regarding Zheng's birth year vary, with some sources dating it to 1595, while others propose 1604 or somewhere in between, like 1600. However, most accounts seem to converge on the year 1604 as the year of his birth. This uncertainty adds an intriguing layer to Zheng's already enigmatic persona.

Furthermore, Zheng's physical appearance was noted to be strikingly handsome, a trait that must have only added to his charismatic presence. His first journey to Japan at the tender age of 18 marks the beginning of his remarkable life journey, a path that would see him navigate through the complexities of his era.

Zheng's journey from a restless teenager to a significant historical figure is a story filled with daring adventures, cultural crossings, and personal transformations. His departure from home as a teenager was the first step in an extraordinary life journey. The reasons for his leaving are shrouded in various tales and speculations. Some sources suggest a scandalous incident, alleging that Zheng had inappropriately touched one of his father's concubines. Others recount a more dramatic version, with his father pursuing him through the streets, stick in hand, in a furious chase. However, these stories, particularly the former, are often dismissed as implausible. It's more likely that Zheng's departure was either a result of his own adventurous spirit or due to his father's frustration with his delinquent behaviors, which reportedly included frequent fighting and vandalism.

Zheng's next destination was Macau, where he sought refuge with his maternal uncle. This move marked a significant turning point in his life. While in Macau, Zheng embraced a new cultural identity, converting to Catholicism and adopting the Christian name Nicholas Gaspard. This conversion was more than a religious shift; it symbolized Zheng's entry into a world that transcended his cultural origins.

In Macau, Zheng's life took another intriguing turn when his uncle entrusted him with a cargo mission to Hirado, Japan. It was here that Zheng met Li Dan, a wealthy and influential Min man who served as the Kapitan Cina, or Chinese headman, of the Japanese city. Li Dan's stature and connections with Europeans presented Zheng with unique opportunities. He found a mentor in Li Dan, who recognized Zheng's linguistic abilities and arranged for him to work as an interpreter for the Dutch. Zheng's proficiency in Portuguese, Chinese, and Japanese made him an invaluable asset in these cross-cultural interactions.

Zheng's skill as a linguist soon led to a critical assignment in 1622. During the conflict between the Ming dynasty and Dutch forces over the Pescadores archipelago, Li Dan sent Zheng to assist in the peace negotiations as a translator. This experience not only deepened Zheng's involvement in significant historical events but also enhanced his understanding of international politics and military strategies.

Amidst these adventures, Zheng's personal life also flourished. Before leaving Japan, he met and married Tagawa Matsu, a local Japanese woman. This marriage was a pivotal moment in Zheng's life, as it led to the birth of his son

Koxinga, whom he conceived with Tagawa Matsu. Zheng left Japan before Koxinga's birth in 1624, setting the stage for his son to become a significant figure in his own right.

The tapestry of Zheng Zhilong's life is interwoven with intriguing alliances, mysterious relationships, and significant transitions, each adding layers to his already complex persona. One such alliance was proposed by the group of traders working closely with the Kapitan Cina, Li Dan. They envisioned a strategic matrimonial union between Zheng and a fellow Chinese woman, Lady Yan. This proposal was not just a matter of personal connection but also a reflection of the intricate social and political networks that Zheng was becoming a part of. Marrying Lady Yan was seen as a move that would further entrench Zheng's position within the influential circles of the Chinese diaspora and their trading enterprises.

However, amidst these well-documented events, there lies a shadowy chapter in Zheng's personal life – the tale of a mysterious daughter born out of wedlock. This alleged daughter, whose existence is shrouded in controversy, is said to have been born to Zheng and a Japanese woman who was not Tagawa Matsu, his known wife. The sole reference to this enigmatic figure comes from the writings of Palafox in his "History of the Conquest of China." Palafox's reliability as a source is highly questionable, casting doubts over the veracity of this claim. According to his account, this daughter was among the Japanese who converted to Christianity, a notable detail given the sociopolitical context of the time.

The narrative becomes even more tangled as Palafox's claims stand in stark contrast to Japanese and Chinese historical accounts, which make no mention of Zheng having such a daughter. The conspicuous absence of any reference to her in these accounts, especially during her teenage years when she would have been more visible, adds to the skepticism surrounding her existence. A speculative theory suggests that this alleged daughter might have been Elizabeth, the daughter of the Kapitan Cina. If this speculation holds any truth, it would imply that Elizabeth was the child of Zheng and the unidentified Japanese woman, assuming the latter even existed.

Zheng's life underwent a dramatic turn following the death of Li Dan in 1625. In the wake of this event, Zheng acquired Li's fleet, a significant development that marked a new chapter in his life. This acquisition was not just a transfer of physical assets but represented a transfer of power, influence, and responsibilities. Zheng's command of the fleet catapulted him into a prominent position in the maritime world of East Asia, setting the stage for his future as a formidable figure in regional politics and trade.

The stories surrounding Zheng Zhilong, ranging from his strategic matrimonial alliances to the mysterious tales of an illegitimate daughter, paint a portrait of a man who was constantly navigating the complex socio-political landscapes of his time.

The rise of Zheng Zhilong to maritime dominance is a saga of intrigue, strategic alliances, and a relentless quest for power. The Dutch East India Company, known as the VOC, had ambitious goals in East Asia. They aimed to secure free trade rights with China and dominate the lucrative trade routes to Japan. To achieve these objectives, they forged an unlikely partnership with Chinese pirates, intending to exert pressure on the Ming dynasty to open up trade. This backdrop sets the stage for Zheng Zhilong's dramatic entry into the world of maritime power struggles.

Zheng initially served as a translator for the Dutch, a role that has stirred some debate among historians. While his early career might seem innocuous, there are suggestions that he might have been involved in pirate activities even then. Despite the uncertainty surrounding his early endeavors, most scholars concur that Zheng eventually joined forces with prominent Chinese pirates, likely figures such as Li Dan or Yan Shiqi. His transition from translator to privateer was formalized in 1624, following the Dutch colonization of Taiwan. During this period, Zheng maintained his alignment with Li Dan.

However, the Dutch, wary of Li Dan's growing influence, devised a plan to use Zheng Zhilong to undermine his position. This strategy, however, was never fully realized due to Li Dan's untimely death. With the demise of Li Dan, Zheng Zhilong emerged as the undisputed leader of the Chinese pirates, a turning point in his life that catapulted him to new heights of power.

Zheng's ascension marked the beginning of a significant expansion and strengthening of his fleets. Leveraging European sailing and military technology, he transformed his armada of junks, making it a formidable force that surpassed even the Chinese Imperial navy in prowess. By 1627, Zheng's fleet had grown to an impressive count of four hundred junks, manned by tens of thousands of men, including Chinese, Japanese, and Europeans. Unique to his command was a personal bodyguard unit composed of former black slaves who had fled from the Portuguese. By 1630, Zheng's influence had grown so vast that he controlled all shipping activities in the South China Sea.

Beyond his naval exploits, Zheng Zhilong also augmented his power through economic strategies. He sold protection passes to fishermen and merchants, ensuring safe passage through the waters he controlled. Such was his dominion that sailing without one of Zheng's passes became unthinkable for fear of retribution. Yet, despite his fearsome reputation, Zheng was not universally despised. In fact, he garnered a considerable amount of admiration from the peasants in the southern provinces of China. His method of governance, which included refraining from unnecessary attacks on their towns and distributing stolen grain during famines, earned him their respect and gratitude. Furthermore, Zheng provided employment opportunities for unemployed fishermen and sailors in his vast fleet, thereby alleviating some of the economic hardships faced by these communities.

The formation of Shibazhi in 1625, under the leadership of Zheng Zhilong, marked a pivotal moment in the maritime history of China. This pirate organization, comprising 18 of the most renowned Chinese pirates, quickly rose to prominence. Among its distinguished members was Shi Daxuan, the father of the notable Shi Lang. The emergence of Shibazhi signaled the beginning of a new era in naval warfare and power dynamics in the region.

Under Zheng's command, Shibazhi swiftly began to challenge the Ming fleet, demonstrating remarkable prowess and strategic acumen. Their approach was not just about brute force; it was a blend of cunning, maritime skills, and an understanding of the political landscape. This formidable pirate coalition won a series of victories, culminating in a significant triumph in 1628, when Zheng Zhilong decisively defeated the Ming dynasty's fleet. This victory was not just a military achievement; it was a turning point that shifted the balance of power in the region. The southern fleet of the Ming dynasty, facing the undeniable strength of Shibazhi, chose to surrender, signaling a dramatic shift in allegiances.

The aftermath of this victory saw Zheng Zhilong at a crossroads. In a surprising turn of events, he decided to transition from his role as a pirate captain to serving the Ming dynasty in an official capacity. His appointment as a major general in 1628 was a testament to his strategic brilliance and his ability to navigate the complex political waters of the time.

A poignant anecdote from this period speaks volumes about Zheng's character and the respect he commanded. It is said that Cai, the governor who had forgiven Zheng years earlier for the mischievous stone-throwing incident, approached Zheng seeking a position in the Ming navy. In a remarkable twist of fate, Zheng, who had once stood before Cai as a mischievous child, now found himself in a position to grant the governor's request. While the authenticity of this story remains uncertain, it captures the essence of Zheng's reputation as a benevolent and magnanimous leader, a narrative that resonated with the people and added to his legendary status.

After aligning his interests with the Ming dynasty, Zheng, along with his wife, chose to establish their base on an island off the coast of Fujian. This location was not just a home; it became the epicenter of Zheng's expansive maritime operations. Commanding a formidable pirate fleet of over 800 ships, his influence extended across a vast expanse, from Japan to Vietnam. His naval prowess and strategic acumen caught the attention of the Chinese Imperial family, leading to his prestigious appointment as the "Admiral of the Coastal Seas." This title was not merely honorary; it was a recognition of Zheng's unmatched control over the maritime territories.

Zheng's role as Admiral was put to a decisive test on October 22, 1633, in the Battle of Liaoluo Bay. In this pivotal encounter, he led his forces against a formidable alliance of Dutch East India Company vessels and renegade junks commanded by Liu Xiang, a former member of the Shibazhi pirates. Zheng's victory in this battle was not just a tactical triumph; it was a strategic masterstroke that significantly bolstered his reputation and influence. The spoils from this victory brought immense wealth to Zheng, transforming him into one of the wealthiest individuals of his time. He used this newfound wealth to acquire a vast expanse of land in Fujian, estimated to be as much as 60% of the province, becoming a powerful and influential landlord.

Even after the fall of the Ming capital Beijing in June 1644, Zheng's loyalty to the Ming dynasty remained unwavering. He continued to serve the dynasty with dedication, even as the political landscape around him shifted dramatically. His brother, Zheng Zhifeng, was honored with the title of marquis under the Southern Ming, though he later faced the formidable challenge of abandoning his post at Zhenjiang due to an overpowering Qing force.

In 1645, following the capture of Nanjing, Zheng's allegiance and skills were once again called upon. He accepted a significant role, being appointed as the commander-in-chief of the imperial forces. His new assignment was to defend the newly established capital in Fuzhou, under the Prince of Tang. This role was not just a military position; it was a symbol of Zheng's unwavering commitment to the Ming cause and a testament to his strategic and leadership abilities.

The year 1646 marked a dramatic and controversial turning point in Zheng Zhilong's life, a decision that would not only alter his fate but also significantly impact the course of Chinese history. In a move that stunned many, Zheng chose to defect to the Manchu Qing forces, an act that had far-reaching consequences. This decision to align with the Manchus led to the abandonment of the strategic passes of Zhejiang, leaving them vulnerable and ultimately facilitating the capture of Fuzhou by Manchu forces. His defection, orchestrated with the assistance of Tong Guozhen and Tong Guoqi, was a calculated move that reflected the complex and often tumultuous political landscape of the time.

However, Zheng's decision to defect was met with staunch resistance from his own family. His brothers, who still wielded considerable control over most of the Zheng army, along with his son Koxinga, vehemently opposed his decision. They implored him not to surrender and to remain loyal to their cause. Despite their pleas, Zheng Zhilong remained steadfast in his decision to defect. This created a rift within his ranks, as his followers and army did not accompany him in his defection. The Qing, noticing this lack of support, grew suspicious of Zheng's loyalty and consequently placed him under house arrest, escorting him to Beijing. In a tragic turn of events, Zheng's loyal bodyguard of former African slaves valiantly fought to protect him but ultimately lost their lives in the attempt to prevent his arrest.

The repercussions of Zheng's defection were not limited to his own fate. The Qing forces marched to his castle in Anhai, targeting his Japanese wife, Tagawa Matsu, in a humiliating and brutal assault. Accounts of what transpired vary, with some stating that Tagawa was violated by Qing forces before she took her own life, while others suggest she committed suicide while bravely directing the fight against the Qing. Regardless of the exact sequence of events, the tragedy of Tagawa Matsu's death further eroded the Qing's trust in Zheng.

Zheng Zhilong's life under house arrest was prolonged and filled with uncertainty. He, along with his servants and sons who had accompanied him, remained confined for many years, until 1661. Initially, the Qing sentenced Zheng and his companions to death by lingchi, an excruciating and protracted form of execution. However, this sentence was later commuted to death by decapitation. Zheng's ultimate fate was sealed as a direct consequence of his son Koxinga's unwavering resistance against the Qing regime. In a final act of retribution, Zheng was executed by the Qing government in 1661 at Caishikou.

Zheng Zhilong's life, marked by meteoric rises, strategic alliances, and a controversial defection, ended in a tragic and ignominious manner. His story is not just a tale of personal ambition and political maneuvering; it is a reflection of the turbulent and transformative period in Chinese history, where loyalty, power, and survival were inextricably intertwined in the complex tapestry of dynastic change and conflict.

George Somers

Sir George Somers, born in the picturesque coastal town of Lyme Regis in Dorset in 1554, was the offspring of John Somers and his wife. From his early years, Somers displayed an extraordinary affinity for the sea, rapidly developing into a renowned seaman known for his exceptional skills. His reputation was not just local; it spread far and wide, as he came to own at least one notable ship, the Julian, which proudly called Lyme Regis its home port.

Somers' maritime career was marked by a series of adventurous exploits, one of the most notable being his first command of the Flibcote. This venture occurred during the tense times of the undeclared Anglo-Spanish War, a period rife with naval skirmishes and bold sea raids. Somers, leading the Flibcote and accompanied by three other vessels, embarked on a daring raid towards Spain. This audacious expedition was not just a display of his nautical prowess but also a testament to his strategic acumen.

The venture culminated in a triumphant return to England, with Somers bringing back Spanish prizes that were a testament to the success of the raid. These prizes were valued at more than £8,000, a substantial sum for that era, signifying a huge economic victory. This feat not only enhanced Somers' stature as a master seaman but also etched his name into the annals of maritime history, marking him as a figure of considerable significance in the narrative of naval warfare between England and Spain.

On May 18th, the voyages of Preston and Somers led them to Dominica. After a brief respite of six days on the island, they journeyed southward to the Los Testigos Islands. There, they held a significant gathering on May 28th before steering southwest to Margarita Island, which they spotted and reached the next day. Their exploration extended to the nearby Coche Island, where they seized a Spanish caravel and captured several pearl fishermen from Puerto Rico, a capture that proved to be of considerable value.

By June 1st, the English fleet, now including eight privateer ships and the captured Spanish vessel, appeared off Cumaná in Spanish Venezuela. Here, they skillfully commandeered three more caravels in the bay. Upon landing, they discovered the locals were forewarned of their arrival. The English then cleverly negotiated a ransom, threatening to burn the town if their demands weren't met. This strategy worked, and they secured a modest haul of foodstuffs from the Spanish. Keeping their word, they departed peacefully the next evening, after setting the captured caravels ablaze.

The English continued their journey along the coastline, anchoring near La Guaira at a beach by Macuto. A small contingent landed and advanced inland, parallel to the sea, until they sighted a fortress guarding La Guaira and the route to Santiago de León de Caracas. Somers then led the main force ashore, and they boldly assaulted the lightly defended fortress of La Guaira, capturing it with minimal resistance. The remaining Spanish garrison fled, alerting nearby forces of the English presence.

The following afternoon, a patrol of fifty Spanish cavaliers from Caracas approached, only to find the English firmly entrenched in the fort. Captain Roberts and his musketeers confronted them, leading to a swift withdrawal by the Spanish. Realizing the English might target Caracas next, the Spanish quickly regrouped to prepare for a possible assault.

The Spanish, in a determined effort to thwart their advance, fortified their positions along the main route to Caracas, known as the King's Highway.

Preston and Somers were well aware of the daunting task ahead. Reaching Caracas, situated significantly inland, presented a formidable challenge, especially as their element of surprise had dissipated. The city, perched on a high plateau at an altitude between 2,500 to 3,000 feet, was nestled within a valley and shielded by the imposing mountains of El Ávila, part of the Venezuelan Coastal Range. The most notable peak on their route, Pico Naiguatá, soared to 9,072 feet, with a topographic isolation of 8,054 feet above sea level. The Caracas garrison, mainly a militia organized by Governor Diego Osorio Villegas, stood ready.

Under the cover of darkness, Preston and Somers led their men out of the fort. They opted for a mountainous path, where detection and engagement by the Spanish would be challenging. The Spanish, perhaps underestimating the English, did not vigilantly monitor their movements, playing into the hands of the English commanders. Moving without rush and aided by the cover of rain, they stealthily navigated through a lesser-known track in the mountains, avoiding the main road.

Guided by a lone indigenous individual, they traversed the densely forested slopes, sometimes having to cut through the thick vegetation. They paused at a stream, refreshing themselves and awaiting dawn. Circling close to the summit of Pico Naiguatá, they descended through the early morning fog and by daylight, they were within view of the town.

To their amazement, by midday on June 8th, they arrived outside Caracas, completely undetected. The six-mile trek through such challenging terrain was a remarkable feat, and astonishingly, they suffered no casualties, only fatigue. A segment of the city's militia was positioned before them, but the majority were still amassed along the main road, unprepared for this unexpected approach.

Preston and Somers swiftly organized their forces into three tactical groups: a primary battle unit in the center and two smaller flanking divisions on each side. The English anticipated a Spanish offensive, but when none came, they launched an attack, effectively driving the Spanish militia to retreat. This skirmish resulted in a single Spanish casualty and several injuries, while the English emerged unscathed.

The militia stationed further up the main road, taken aback by the sudden onslaught, descended into chaos and were unable to mount an effective defense. Consequently, the English troops faced minimal resistance as they entered the city, with most non-combatants having already fled. The governor, Diego de Osorio, was absent, leaving the defense to the mayor of Baruta, an elderly Spanish rider named Alonso Andrea de Ledesma. Despite his valiant attempt with lance and shield, Ledesma was fatally shot. In recognition of his bravery, Preston instructed that Ledesma be honored as a hero and buried with respect. By 3pm, the English had secured control over Caracas.

The English occupation lasted five days. During negotiations for the city's ransom, the English initially demanded 30,000 ducats, but the Spanish countered with offers of 2,000 and then 3,000 ducats. Dissatisfied, Preston and Somers began looting the city. A final ransom offer of 4,000 ducats was proposed to spare what remained of the town. However, intelligence from indigenous sources revealed that the Spanish were stalling for time, awaiting reinforcements. Enraged by this perceived deceit, the English set Caracas and some nearby settlements ablaze the following morning.

Retreating along their previous route, they managed to evade the now-reinforced Spanish militia and returned to La Guaira by noon on June 14th, laden with plunder but exhausted. The next day, Preston and Somers set the fortress and its defenses ablaze, finalizing their preparations to depart. The Spanish militia re-entered Caracas shortly after the English departure, only to find the city largely reduced to ruins.

The following day, the English forces left La Guaira and proceeded westward.

By June 16th, they reached the vicinity of Chichiriviche. Here, Somers led a detachment in a small boat operation, successfully capturing three Spanish vessels at anchor. They swiftly confiscated the valuables from these ships before setting them ablaze. The town of Chichiriviche, upon their entry, offered little resistance, but its small size rendered the prospect of a ransom unfeasible. Consequently, the English moved further west, setting their sights on Santa Ana de Coro.

On June 20th, as they navigated along the coast, the English spotted Coro Bay. Preston, commanding the operation, efficiently organized the landing of all his troops by 11 p.m. Their objective was the town of Coro, situated at the southern end of the Paraguaná Peninsula on a coastal plain, bordered by the sandy Médanos Isthmus. This area held historical significance, having been colonized by Germans in the 1520s to 1540s as part of an arrangement with the Spanish. Coro was defended by a modest garrison, under the command of Governor Juan de Riberos.

While Somers remained with fifty men to secure the anchorage, the Spanish quickly became aware of their presence and mobilized their militia to confront them. During a nighttime assault on the town, the English forces encountered a robust barricade erected by the Spaniards, hindering their initial advance. Despite a forceful attack, the English were initially repelled by the determined Spanish defenders. Attempts to outflank the barricade also met with failure, and the English started to incur losses.

However, reinforced by additional troops, the English mounted another attack, eventually breaking through the defenses and driving the Spanish defenders back. This led to a skirmish where the English pursued the retreating Spaniards, overcoming only minor delays in their advance. By the following morning, they had successfully taken control of Coro with relatively few casualties. The town, however, was largely deserted, as its residents, along with Governor de Riberos, had been forewarned of the impending attack and had fled inland, taking their valuables with them. Preston then ordered the town to be thoroughly looted.

Coro remained under English control for approximately two days. During this time, Preston learned of a storm that had struck their anchorage, causing the cables of Somers's fifty-man pinnace to snap and the vessel to be driven out to sea. In response, Preston commanded a thorough sacking and burning of Coro, including its church and chapel.

Preston quickly organized his troops for a return to the coast, intent on setting sail to locate Somers. By the evening of their departure, Somers was found near the entrance to Lake Maracaibo, seeking refuge. However, with the wind conditions favoring their departure, both parties decided to leave, setting a course for Hispaniola with the wind at their backs on June 26th.

By June 30th, the squadron led by Preston and Somers had reached the vicinity of Hispaniola, and on the following day, they anchored off Cape Tiburón to replenish their supplies. However, when they resumed their journey on July 8th, only Preston's Ascension and Somers's Gift remained in the formation, as the other ships had decided to return to England.

A few days later, on July 12th, the remaining privateer vessels arrived off the coast of Jamaica. After a brief stay, they continued their voyage towards the Cayman Islands. By July 22nd, they had reached Cabo Corrientes in Cuba, where they attempted to establish a temporary blockade off Havana with the hope of capturing a few small vessels as prizes. However, their success was limited, managing to capture only two small ships.

During this period, the crews were ravaged by disease, with dysentery claiming the lives of eighty men. Given the rising toll of illness and the limited success in capturing prizes, the decision was made to terminate the expedition. Fortunate to have avoided significant damage from Spanish forces and not wishing to push their luck further, Preston and Somers set a course back to England, concluding their venture.

In 1609, Sir George Somers was appointed as the admiral of a relief fleet organized by the Virginia Company. This Third Supply mission was intended to aid the Jamestown colony in North America, which had been established two years earlier. On June 2, 1609, Somers embarked from Plymouth on the Sea Venture, the flagship of a fleet consisting of seven ships, along with two additional pinnaces in tow. This fleet was tasked with transporting 500 to 600 colonists to Jamestown, Virginia.

However, on July 25, the fleet encountered a severe storm, likely a hurricane, leading to the separation of the ships. The Sea Venture, under Somers' command, battled the storm for three days. While similar-sized ships had survived such conditions, the Sea Venture was at a disadvantage due to her recent construction; her timbers had not yet fully set. This flaw became apparent as the caulking was forced out, causing the ship to leak significantly. Despite relentless bailing efforts by the crew, water continued to rise in the hold. In a desperate attempt to lighten the ship and increase buoyancy, her guns were jettisoned, a measure which only provided a temporary reprieve.

Admiral Somers, who personally took the helm during the storm, sighted land on the morning of July 28. By this time, the ship was critically flooded, with nine feet of water in the hold and the crew and passengers pushed to the brink of exhaustion. In a decisive move to save the lives aboard, Somers deliberately ran the ship aground on the reefs of what turned out to be Bermuda. This act of quick thinking ensured the safety of all 150 people, including a dog, as they managed to reach shore at what they would later call Discovery Bay.

The rest of the fleet, having lost sight of the Sea Venture and enduring the damaging effects of the storm themselves, assumed that Somers and his crew had perished. Little did they know, Somers and his passengers had survived, albeit stranded on the shores of Bermuda.

For 10 months, Somers and his shipwrecked company found themselves marooned in Bermuda. They survived by consuming the island's natural resources and fishing from the surrounding sea. This extraordinary event is believed by some scholars to have been the inspiration for William Shakespeare's play "The Tempest."

During their unexpected sojourn in Bermuda, the shipwreck survivors constructed a church and several houses, laying the foundations of what would become the Bermuda colony. Under the leadership of Somers and Sir Thomas Gates, they embarked on an ambitious project to build two new ships, the Deliverance and the Patience, using Bermuda Cedar and materials salvaged from the Sea Venture.

In May 1610, these newly constructed vessels, carrying the 142 survivors and provisions from the island, set sail for Jamestown. Upon their arrival, they discovered a settlement ravaged by famine and disease during the period known as the "Starving Time." The hurricane that had ensnared the Sea Venture had also impacted the rest of the Supply Relief Fleet, resulting in a dire shortage of supplies at the colony, with only 60 settlers clinging to life. The timely arrival of the Deliverance and the Patience, laden with food from Bermuda, along with a subsequent relief fleet led by Lord Delaware in July 1610, proved crucial in sustaining the colony and preventing the abandonment of Jamestown.

After ensuring the survival of the Jamestown settlers, Somers returned to Bermuda aboard the Patience to gather more provisions. However, during this voyage, he fell ill and passed away in Bermuda on November 9, 1610, at the age of 56. Legend has it that Somers, having developed a deep affection for Bermuda, requested that his heart be buried on the island. A memorial in Somers' Gardens in St. George's commemorates the approximate location of his heart's burial. The remainder of his body was transported back to England for burial in Whitchurch Canonicorum, near Lyme Regis, the town of his birth.

Robert Searle

The enigmatic origins of the notorious buccaneer, whose name echoes through the annals of maritime history, remain shrouded in mystery. The revered chronicler of buccaneer lore, Esquemeling, claimed that this formidable pirate was "born at Jamaica." However, this assertion casts a shadow of doubt, considering Jamaica only fell under English rule in 1655. Delving deeper into his life reveals a tumultuous career marked by the intriguing dichotomy of being a "gentleman of fortune." His path was consistently intertwined with conflicts and disagreements with Sir Thomas Modyford, the royal governor of Jamaica. Modyford, known for his unusual camaraderie with buccaneers, often found himself at odds with this particular pirate. The tumultuous relationship between the buccaneer and the governor paints a vivid picture of the complex dynamics within the pirate world, where alliances were as unpredictable as the Caribbean seas.

In 1659, the seas bore witness to a riveting chapter of maritime history with the capture of the Cagway, a formidable 60-ton, 8-gun vessel, during an audacious raid led by the legendary Sir Christopher Myngs. This vessel, the largest of four Spanish merchantmen seized in the daring operation against Santa Marta and Tolú in Colombia, marked the rise of a new maritime force. Four years later, in 1662, the Cagway, under the skilled leadership of Captain Searle, joined Myng's formidable expedition aimed at the strategic heart of the Spanish empire, Santiago de Cuba. This formidable fleet, comprising a dozen vessels and a robust force of 1,300 men, embarked from the bustling Port Royal in Jamaica on the 1st of October. After navigating the treacherous

Caribbean waters for two and a half weeks, they made a strategic landing east of Santiago, swiftly overpowering the city the following day and seizing a considerable treasure, which was triumphantly carried back to Jamaica.

However, the winds of fortune were shifting by 1664. The political climate in Europe and the Caribbean was simmering with tension and unpredictability. The continuous and ruthless raids by English buccaneers had sparked a series of vehement protests from Madrid, directly to King Charles II of England. In a stark response, King Charles penned a stern letter to Governor Modyford of Jamaica, articulating his profound dissatisfaction with the relentless acts of violence and depredation against the Spanish. The king's directive was unequivocal: halt these aggressions immediately, punish the perpetrators severely, and ensure full restitution to the victims.

This letter, signed in London and dispatched 11 days after Modyford's arrival at Port Royal in early June, did not reach its destination until September. Its arrival sent shockwaves through the island, particularly as two lucrative Spanish prizes from Cuba were docked at Port Royal, heavily guarded and under Searle's command. With the Spanish loot already ashore for the king's inspection, Modyford hastily convened the Council of Jamaica to deliberate on this pressing matter.

The Council, alarmed by the king's edict, acted swiftly, deciding to inform the governor of Cuba that the seized ships and wealth would be returned. A resolution was passed, branding any future acts of aggression against the Spanish as piracy and rebellion. As a decisive measure, Captain Searle's commission was revoked, and his ship was effectively immobilized by removing its rudder and sails.

In the tumultuous year of 1665, as the Second Anglo-Dutch War ignited, the tides of fate turned once more for Captain Searle. His ship, once immobilized, was revitalized with its rudder and sails reattached, ready to set sail on new adventures. The early months of 1666 saw Searle and his crew join a formidable fleet assembled by the renowned Colonel Edward Morgan, uncle to the infamous Sir Henry Morgan. This expedition, composed of nine ships and a crew of 650 soldiers, had its sights set on the Dutch islands of Sint Eustatius and Sabá. Governor Modyford, in a detailed letter, vividly described this force as an assembly of "chiefly reformed privateers," a band of resolute and heavily armed men, veterans of the sea, bearing fusils and pistols.

Modyford expressed his satisfaction with this expedition, noting its economical nature. The governor remarked on the "old rate of no purchase, no pay" policy, pointing out the minimal cost to the Crown, with only some powder and mortar pieces being the main expenditure. This arrangement highlighted the enterprising spirit of the time, where privateering was a venture driven by the promise of plunder.

However, tragedy struck this ambitious venture. Upon their successful landing, Colonel Morgan, a man of substantial corpulence, succumbed to the intense heat. In his eagerness to engage the enemy, he overexerted himself, leading to his untimely demise. This unexpected turn of events was marked by the poignant image of the valiant colonel, overcome by the elements in his pursuit of victory.

Despite their initial success, the English force soon faced internal strife. Discord arose over the division of meager spoils and disputes regarding the successor to the late Colonel Morgan, leading to the disintegration of their united front.

In the following year, 1667, Captain Searle, alongside Captain Stedman, embarked on another audacious endeavor. Commanding two small ships and a crew of 80 men, they set their sights on the Dutch island of Tobago, near Trinidad. This raid was marked by its thoroughness, as they sacked the island from end to end. Concurrently, Lord Willoughby, the governor of the English colony of Barbados, had also organized an expedition to capture Tobago. However, Searle's Jamaican contingent, ever the opportunists, beat them to the punch, arriving three to four days earlier.

As Willoughby's forces arrived, they found Searle and his men in the midst of their plundering spree. A tense negotiation ensued, where Willoughby, asserting his authority, demanded the island in the name of the king. The buccaneers, pragmatic in their approach, agreed to leave the fort and governor's house untouched. This concession, however, came with a condition: they demanded the liberty to sell their hard-won booty in Barbados.

In June of 1667, amidst the turbulent waves of Caribbean politics, Governor Modyford of Jamaica took a decisive stand. He issued a sweeping proclamation that forbade further privateering raids and recalled all commissions issued in Jamaica. This edict, however, soon brought him face-to-face with the notorious Robert Searle, a man whose recent actions demanded retribution.

The backdrop of this confrontation was a dramatic series of events. Following Sir Henry Morgan's notorious raid on Maracaibo in Venezuela, Searle found himself in New Providence in the Bahamas. It was here that a Spanish retaliatory force struck, attacking the English settlement with a vengeance. This incursion ignited a fierce response from the privateersmen, including Searle, who, fueled by anger and a thirst for retribution, set their course for Florida. In May 1668, they launched a bold raid on the presidio of St. Augustine. This act of retaliation, however, came in direct defiance of Modyford's recent proclamation.

Searle's raid had a significant outcome: it facilitated the escape of Henry Woodward, the first settler of South Carolina, who had been a captive of the Spanish at St. Augustine. Woodward's freedom marked a turning point in his life, as he went on to serve as a surgeon on privateer ships for several years.

Upon his return to Jamaica, Searle was well aware of his precarious position. Rather than boldly entering Port Royal, he strategically anchored the Cagway in a secluded bay at the southwestern end of the island, staying out of the governor's immediate reach. Modyford, in his report to Lord Arlington, England's Secretary of State, conveyed the situation with a sense of urgency:

"There arrived also at Port Morant the Cagway, Captain Searle, with 70 stout men, who hearing that I was much incensed against him for that action of St. Augustine, went to Macary Bay, and there rides out of command. I will use the best ways to apprehend him, without driving his men to despair."

The tension escalated when Searle, perhaps underestimating the governor's resolve, ventured ashore. He was promptly seized by Modyford's forces and placed under arrest in Port Royal. The weeks that followed were filled with anticipation and uncertainty. Modyford penned another letter to Arlington, detailing that Searle was still in the custody of Jamaica's Provost Marshal, awaiting trial. The island buzzed with rumors and speculation about the fate of the bold privateer, a man who had dared to defy the governor's orders and had paid the price for his audacity.

In a twist of fate that highlighted the unpredictable nature of the buccaneer's life, Robert Searle found himself freed from his confinement, not due to clemency but because of his skills needed in a grand endeavor. He was to play a crucial role in one of the most epic land battles of buccaneering history: Sir Henry Morgan's infamous sack of Panama City. Searle, elevated to the status of one of Morgan's trusted lieutenants, was tasked with a mission of great strategic importance — to prevent any Spanish ships from fleeing the port during the assault.

As the battle unfolded, Searle and his men made a pivotal discovery at the port. They stumbled upon a barque, grounded and smoldering, an apparent victim of a hasty Spanish attempt to prevent its capture. With swift action, the buccaneers extinguished the flames, salvaging a vessel that would soon prove to be an invaluable prize. In the following days, Searle's tenacity and naval prowess shone through as he captured three additional ships, forming a small but formidable flotilla.

Commanding this fleet, Searle embarked on a relentless pursuit across the nearby islands — Perico, Taboga, Tobogilla, Otoque, and the outer reaches of the Pearl Islands. His target was the hapless refugees who had sought shelter there. This campaign was ruthless and effective, resulting in the capture of numerous prisoners and a substantial haul of property. Don Juan Pérez de Guzmán, the President of Panama, lamented in his writings the significant damage inflicted by the English, particularly emphasizing the critical role of the barque that had been saved from destruction.

Searle's primary objective was the interception of ships laden with valuables, rumored to be concealed in various anchorages along the Panama coast and among the islands. His search led him to Taboga, where an unexpected discovery awaited him and his crew. Hidden amidst the foliage, they found a substantial cache of Peruvian wine. The discovery proved too tempting for the weary seamen. As they indulged in the unexpected bounty, the evening descended into a raucous celebration, leaving most of the crew helplessly inebriated.

Under the cloak of a moonless night, a band of buccaneers, their senses dulled by copious amounts of rum, reveled on a secluded beach. In their drunken revelry, they failed to notice the stealthy approach of a Spanish galleon, the Santissima Trinidad, slicing through the dark waters toward them. This massive vessel, a 400-ton leviathan of the sea, came to anchor unnoticed, its presence as silent as a shadow.

In the midst of their carousing, the pirates remained oblivious to a small boat being quietly lowered from the galleon, rowed toward the shore with a cargo of casks. It was only by a stroke of serendipity, or perhaps fate, that the pirates stumbled upon the boat's seven-man crew, who had landed in search of fresh water. These Spaniards, taken aback by their sudden capture, found themselves at the mercy of the pirates and their notorious leader, Searle.

Under the threat of torture, the captured crew revealed the astonishing truth: their ship, the Santissima Trinidad, was a floating treasury, laden with the King's Plate, an opulent bounty of gold, pearls, and jewels. This treasure was not just the wealth of Panama's elite; it also included the precious belongings of religious women from the city's nunnery. These women, in their flight, had brought with them the sacred ornaments of their church, a trove of gold and precious artifacts of immense value.

Remarkably, this single ship, reported to be only modestly armed with seven cannons and a dozen muskets, and poorly provisioned with food and water, was tasked with the monumental responsibility of safeguarding the collective wealth of the government, private citizens, and the Church in Panama. It was a desperate bid to protect their riches from the marauding buccaneers.

The captain of this laden vessel, Don Francisco de Peralta, had eschewed the expected course to Lima, Peru, instead braving the open sea. His plan, it seemed, was to outwait the pirates, believing they had no means to pursue him at sea. His intention was to return to Panama, cargo and passengers unharmed, once the buccaneer threat had subsided. Little did he know, his ship had sailed straight into the lion's den, a twist of fate that would irrevocably entangle the destinies of the pirates and the occupants of the Santissima Trinidad.

In the wake of the Spaniards' capture, Robert Searle, with the urgency of a commander sensing imminent glory, issued a command to his men: seize the galleon at all costs. Yet, his orders fell on deaf ears, drowned out by the raucous revelry and the intoxicating allure of wine. The buccaneers, either too engrossed in their drunken merriment or physically incapacitated, failed to muster the strength to pursue the grand prize that lay within their grasp.

Meanwhile, Captain Don Francisco de Peralta, growing increasingly anxious over the absence of his men and suspicious of the nearby barque, made a critical decision. With considerable effort, he commanded his crew to weigh anchor, and under the cloak of darkness, the Santissima Trinidad made a stealthy retreat, vanishing into the night's embrace, well out of sight by the break of dawn.

This missed opportunity only came to light among the main body of buccaneers a few days later, sparking a fury like no other. Esquemeling, even years after the event, recounted with evident disdain how Searle, preoccupied with his captives, notably a group of Spanish women, had squandered a golden chance. Instead of launching an immediate pursuit of the treasure-laden ship, Searle chose to indulge in drink and frivolity. This lapse in judgment earned him severe reproach from his fellow buccaneer, Morgan, and resulted in a permanent rift in their relationship.

Years later, in a twist of fate, Captain de Peralta encountered the English privateer William Dampier in the Pacific. During his captivity, de Peralta regaled his captor with the tale of his narrow escape from Searle, a story he recounted with a mixture of pride and relief.

As for Robert Searle, his life took him to Honduras, where he met a fate as dramatic as his life had been. William Dampier, chronicling the buccaneer's end, wrote of Searle's demise in a duel with an Indigenous logwood cutter. This encounter, taking place near a small sandy islet at the northern end of the Gulf of Campeache, in the Laguna de Términos, marked the end of the infamous Jamaican buccaneer. The islet, known among pirates as "Searle's Key," earned its name from Captain Searle himself, who had once careened his vessel there. It was in the Western Lagune, while cutting logwood with a member of his crew, that Searle met his unexpected end, thus closing the chapter on a life woven with adventure, treachery, and the relentless pursuit of fortune.

Henry Morgan

orn around 1635 in Wales, possibly in Llanrumney or Pencarn, both in Monmouthshire, Harri Morgan's early life is shrouded in historical ambiguity. While some sources, including David Williams in the Dictionary of Welsh Biography, note the difficulty in accurately tracing Morgan's lineage, it is often suggested that his father was Robert Morgan, a local farmer. This uncertainty extends to his early education and career choices. According to Nuala Zahedieh's entry in the Oxford Dictionary of National Biography, Morgan himself later claimed that he had abandoned formal education early, favoring martial pursuits over academic ones, stating he was "much more used to the pike than the book."

The trajectory that led Morgan to the Caribbean remains a subject of speculation. One theory posits his arrival with the army of Robert Venables, dispatched by Oliver Cromwell during the 1654 Caribbean expedition against the Spanish in the West Indies. Alternatively, it is conjectured that Morgan might have journeyed there as an apprentice to a cutlery maker, trading three years of service for the cost of his passage. Richard Browne, a surgeon who worked under Morgan in 1670, suggested that Morgan could have arrived as a "private gentleman" after the English captured Jamaica in 1655 or, more dramatically, he might have been abducted in Bristol and sold as a servant in Barbados.

The Caribbean in the 17th century was a land of opportunity and peril. For ambitious young men like Morgan, it promised rapid wealth, especially through the burgeoning sugar export economy, which required substantial investment for high returns. Another lucrative avenue was through trade or the plundering of the Spanish Empire. Privateering played a significant role in this era, with individuals and ships commissioned by governments to attack and seize assets from enemy nations. Morgan's journey into this volatile and opportunity-rich environment set the stage for his eventual rise to notoriety.

In the early 1660s, during England's war with Spain, Harri Morgan likely joined the ranks of privateers under the leadership of Sir Christopher Myngs. This group was notorious for their attacks on Spanish cities and settlements across the Caribbean and Central America. Around 1663, Morgan is believed to have commanded a ship within Myngs' fleet, participating in notable assaults such as the attack on Santiago de Cuba and the infamous Sack of Campeche on the Yucatán Peninsula.

Sir Thomas Modyford, appointed as the Governor of Jamaica in February 1664, initially received orders to curb the activities of these privateers. He issued a proclamation against their operations on June 11, 1664. However, the economic realities of the time led to a swift reversal of this policy by the end of the same month. Jamaica, at that time, hosted approximately 1,500 privateers who significantly contributed to the island's revenue stream. This financial influx was vital for the sustenance of the island's nascent planting community, which numbered around 5,000 people. Without the economic boost provided by the privateers, Jamaica faced the risk of an economic collapse.

Privateers, like Morgan, operated under a letter of marque—a formal license authorizing them to attack and seize vessels, typically those of a specified country, under certain conditions. These actions were not just acts of piracy but were sanctioned by the government, and a portion of the spoils obtained was customarily allocated to the sovereign or the issuing authority. This legal framework allowed privateers to operate on the fringes of legality, contribut-ing to their controversial but crucial role in the geopolitical landscape of the

17th century Caribbean.

In August 1665, Harri Morgan, alongside fellow captains John Morris and Jacob Fackman, made a triumphant return to Port Royal, laden with a substantial cargo of treasures. Their success caught the attention of Sir Thomas Modyford, the Governor of Jamaica, who was so impressed by the haul that he reported back to the government, highlighting Central America as an ideal target for further attacks on the Spanish Indies.

The next two years of Morgan's life are somewhat veiled in history, but a significant personal event occurred in early 1666 when he married his cousin, Mary Morgan, the daughter of Edward Morgan, Jamaica's Deputy Governor. This union elevated Henry into the upper echelons of Jamaican society, although the couple did not have any children.

The onset of hostilities between the English and Dutch in 1664 led to a shift in colonial policy. Governors were now authorized to issue letters of marque against the Dutch. Despite this new directive, many privateers, including Morgan, were hesitant to engage with the Dutch. An expedition aimed at capturing the Dutch island of Sint Eustatius tragically resulted in the death of Morgan's father-in-law, who was commanding a 600-man force.

Historical accounts vary regarding Morgan's activities in 1666. H. R. Allen, in his biography of Morgan, suggests that the privateer served as second-in-command to Captain Edward Mansvelt. Mansvelt, armed with a letter of marque for the invasion of Curaçao, ultimately refrained from attacking Willemstad, the island's main city, either due to its formidable defenses or a lack of sufficient plunder. On the other hand, historians Jan Rogoziński and Stephan Talty note that during this time, Morgan was preoccupied with overseeing the Port Royal militia and fortifying Jamaica's defenses. His leadership contributed to the partial construction of Fort Charles at Port Royal. Around this period, Morgan also made a significant investment in his future by purchasing his first plantation in Jamaica.

In 1667, as tensions escalated between England and Spain, rumors of a potential Spanish invasion began to stir in Jamaica. Reacting to these concerns, Governor Sir Thomas Modyford authorized the privateers to act against Spain and issued Harri Morgan a letter of marque. This document tasked Morgan with rallying the English privateers to capture Spanish prisoners and gather intelligence about the purported plans to attack Jamaica. Modyford appointed Morgan as admiral, and by January 1668, Morgan had mustered a fleet of 10 ships and 500 men, later reinforced by an additional 2 ships and 200 men from Tortuga, now part of Haiti.

Morgan's letter of marque explicitly allowed him to target Spanish ships at sea, without the authority for land-based attacks. The spoils from these sea raids were to be divided between the government and the ship owners. However, if the privateers exceeded their mandate and raided cities, they could keep all the loot for themselves. Historian Jan Rogoziński notes that while city raids were technically acts of illegal piracy, they were immensely profitable. Nuala Zahedieh suggests that such attacks could be justified if Morgan provided evidence of an imminent Spanish assault.

Initially aiming to attack Havana, Morgan diverted to Puerto del Príncipe (now Camagüey), a town located inland, upon learning of Havana's strong defenses. The raid on Puerto del Príncipe yielded less treasure than anticipated, leading to widespread disappointment among Morgan's crew. Alexandre Exquemelin, a crew member, recorded their frustration at the modest haul. Upon reporting back to Modyford, Morgan claimed to have discovered evidence of Spanish preparations for an assault on British territories, including the mobilization of forces from various locations to converge at Santiago de Cuba.

Following this operation, a conflict erupted among Morgan's crew when an English privateer fatally stabbed a French shipmate. To prevent an outbreak of violence between the English and French sailors, Morgan apprehended the assailant and vowed to the French that the English sailor would face execution upon their return to Port Royal. True to his word, Morgan ensured the sailor was hanged.

After the raid on Puerto del Príncipe, Harri Morgan set his sights on Porto Bello, now in modern Panama, known as one of the largest and most fortified cities on the Spanish Main. The city, a crucial hub in the trade network between the Spanish territories and Spain, was heavily guarded, protected by two castles in the harbor and another within the city itself.

However, the division of spoils from the previous conquest led to discontent among the 200 French privateers in Morgan's crew, further exacerbated by the incident involving the murder of a French crew member. Dissatisfied, these French privateers left Morgan and returned to Tortuga. Undeterred, Morgan and his remaining forces made a brief stop at Port Royal before embarking towards Porto Bello.

On July 11, 1668, Morgan's fleet anchored near Porto Bello. The men were transferred to 23 canoes and silently paddled to a landing point close to the city. Approaching the first castle from land, they launched a pre-dawn assault and swiftly captured all three castles and the town. Despite the victory, the privateers suffered casualties, with 18 men lost and 32 wounded. Historian Nuala Zahedieh remarks on Morgan's military prowess, noting the operation at Porto Bello as a testament to his strategic acumen and precise timing.

Alexandre Exquemelin, who documented these events, described a controversial tactic used by Morgan during the siege. To breach the third castle, Morgan allegedly ordered the construction of wide ladders to accommodate three men abreast. He then forced captured religious figures to carry these ladders and lead the assault, resulting in many casualties among them. This account, particularly the use of nuns and monks as shields, sparked controversy. Terry Breverton, in his biography of Morgan, notes that when Exquemelin's book was later translated and published in England, Morgan sued for libel and won. This specific allegation about the use of religious figures as human shields was retracted in subsequent English editions of the book.

Morgan and his crew occupied Porto Bello for a month, during which he demanded a ransom of 350,000 pesos from Don Agustín, the acting president of Panama, for the city's release. While they plundered the city, it is likely that they resorted to torture to extract information about hidden treasures. However, historian Nuala Zahedieh notes that there are no first-hand witness accounts to substantiate Alexandre Exquemelin's claims of widespread rape and debauchery during this period.

An attempt by Don Agustín to retake the city with an 800-strong army failed against Morgan's privateers. Eventually, a negotiated ransom of 100,000 pesos was agreed upon. After collecting the ransom and looting the city, Morgan and his men returned to Port Royal, carrying an estimated £70,000 to £100,000 in cash and valuables. Zahedieh points out that this sum surpassed the agricultural output of Jamaica and nearly equaled half of Barbados's sugar exports. Each privateer received around £120, an amount five to six times the average annual earnings of a sailor at that time. Morgan himself earned a five percent share for his role, while Governor Modyford, who had issued Morgan's letter of marque, received a ten percent share.

Despite Morgan having exceeded the limits of his commission, Modyford reported back to London that he had reprimanded Morgan for his actions. However, in Britain, Morgan was celebrated as a national hero, and neither he nor Modyford faced any significant repercussions for their actions.

Shortly after his return to Port Royal, Harri Morgan embarked on another venture in October 1668, setting sail with a fleet of ten ships and 800 men to Île-à-Vache, a small island serving as his gathering point. His ambitious target was Cartagena de Indias, the wealthiest and most pivotal city on the Spanish Main. In December, Morgan's fleet was bolstered by the addition of the former Royal Navy frigate, Oxford, which had been dispatched to Port Royal to assist in any defense of Jamaica. Governor Modyford subsequently reassigned Oxford to Morgan, who made it his flagship.

A dramatic turn of events unfolded on January 2, 1669, during a council of war aboard the Oxford. A spark ignited the ship's powder magazine, resulting in a catastrophic explosion that destroyed the vessel and claimed the lives of over 200 crew members. Miraculously, Morgan and the captains seated on one side of the table were catapulted into the water and survived, while the four captains seated opposite perished.

The destruction of the Oxford significantly weakened Morgan's fleet, rendering an assault on Cartagena infeasible. Instead, a French captain under his command suggested replicating the earlier exploits of the pirate François l'Olonnais by targeting Maracaibo and Gibraltar, both located on Lake Maracaibo in present-day Venezuela. The French captain was familiar with the narrow, shallow channel leading to the lagoon. Since l'Olonnais's visit, the Spanish had constructed the San Carlos de la Barra Fortress near Maracaibo, ostensibly a strong defensive position. However, historian Stephan Talty notes that the fortress was inadequately manned, with only nine soldiers to operate its 11 guns.

Morgan's approach was covered by cannon fire from his flagship, Lilly. The privateers landed on the beach and stormed the fort, only to find it deserted. They soon discovered a slow-burning fuse leading to the fort's powder kegs, left by the Spanish as a trap, which Morgan promptly extinguished. To prevent the fortress's guns from being used against them upon their return, the privateers spiked and buried them before continuing with their mission.

Upon reaching Maracaibo, Morgan found it largely abandoned, as the inhabitants had been warned of his arrival by the troops from the fortress. Over three weeks, Morgan and his crew ransacked the city. To locate hidden treasures, they scoured the surrounding jungle for escapees and subjected some of the remaining residents to torture.

After exhausting Maracaibo's resources, Morgan set his sights on Gibraltar, located further south across Lake Maracaibo. The town's defenders initially resisted, managing to keep Morgan's forces at bay with a barrage from their fort. Morgan, however, chose a strategic approach, anchoring at a distance and sending his men in canoes to attack from land. They encountered minimal resistance, as many inhabitants had already fled into the jungle. Morgan's stay in Gibraltar lasted five weeks, and, as in Maracaibo, there are indications that torture was employed to extract information about hidden valuables.

Four days after leaving Maracaibo, Morgan returned to find the Armada de Barlovento, a Spanish defense squadron commanded by Don Alonso del Campo y Espinosa, blocking the passage between the Caribbean and Lake Maracaibo. The Spaniards, armed with 126 cannons and having re-armed the San Carlos de la Barra Fortress, were under orders to eradicate piracy in the region. Negotiations ensued for a week, with Espinosa demanding that Morgan leave behind all spoils and slaves in exchange for safe passage back to Jamaica. No agreement was reached that would allow Morgan and his crew to retain their loot without facing attack.

Faced with this dilemma, Morgan presented the Spanish offers to his men, who voted to fight their way through. Outnumbered and outgunned, one privateer proposed the use of a fire ship aimed at Espinosa's flagship, Magdalen. To execute this plan, a crew of 12 prepared a captured ship from Gibraltar. They ingeniously disguised vertical logs with headwear to simulate a crew and cut extra portholes in the hull, inserting logs to mimic cannons. Barrels of gunpowder were placed aboard, and grappling irons were woven into the ship's rigging to ensnare Magdalen's ropes and sails, ensuring the two ships would become entangled.

On May 1, 1669, Morgan launched his attack on the Spanish squadron. The ingenious fire ship strategy proved effective, swiftly setting Espinosa's flagship, Magdalen, ablaze. Espinosa was forced to abandon his ship and retreated to the fort, where he continued to oversee the battle. The second-largest Spanish ship, Soledad, encountered rigging problems and drifted aimlessly until privateers boarded, repaired it, and seized it as plunder. The privateers also sunk the third Spanish vessel in the squadron.

Morgan still faced the challenge of passing the well-armed San Carlos de la Barra Fortress. The fortress's cannons posed a significant threat to his fleet, capable of obliterating it if they attempted to pass. Morgan opted for negotiation, threatening to sack and burn Maracaibo if passage was not granted. While Espinosa refused to negotiate, the citizens of Maracaibo, fearing for their city, agreed to pay 20,000 pesos and provide 500 head of cattle in exchange for Morgan's restraint. Concurrently, Morgan's men salvaged 15,000 pesos from the wreck of Magdalen.

Before proceeding, Morgan distributed the loot equally among his ships, totaling 250,000 pesos, along with a vast amount of merchandise and a number of slaves, to mitigate the risk of losing everything if a single ship were sunk.

Morgan then exploited Espinosa's tactical oversight. Observing that the Spanish cannons were positioned for a landward attack, the privateers feigned a landing. As the Spanish forces redeployed to repel an expected night assault, Morgan's fleet silently raised anchor, using the tide to maneuver past the fortress before unfurling their sails. They successfully escaped to Port Royal unscathed, a move that historian Nuala Zahedieh describes as demonstrating Morgan's characteristic cunning and audacity.

During Morgan's absence, a pro-Spanish faction had influenced King Charles II, leading to a shift in English foreign policy. Upon Morgan's return, Governor Modyford reprimanded him for actions beyond his commission and revoked the letters of marque. However, no official action was taken against the privateers. Morgan, with his share of the prize money, invested in an 836-acre plantation, his second such investment, further entrenching his status and wealth in the region.

Queen Mariana of Spain, infuriated by Morgan's audacious attacks, retaliated by ordering the seizure or destruction of all English ships in the Caribbean. The first of these retaliatory actions occurred in March 1670, when Spanish privateers, including Manuel Ribeiro Pardal operating under a letter of marque, began targeting English trade ships. In response, Governor Modyford commissioned Morgan to undertake any necessary actions to ensure the safety and peace of Jamaica.

Meanwhile, a tragic incident unfolded aboard the Oxford. While Morgan and visiting captains were celebrating on Île à Vache, a spark accidentally ignited the ship's magazine, resulting in a catastrophic explosion that killed over 200 people. Miraculously, Morgan and six other captains, seated on one side of the table, survived, while those on the opposite side perished.

Undeterred by this disaster, Morgan began planning his next venture in April 1670. Ambitiously aiming to capture a significant Spanish port, he realized the need for a substantial force and initiated an extensive recruitment drive. He reached out to the English in Jamaica and the French in Tortuga and Hispaniola, aware that this expedition might be his last due to the looming inevitability of peace with Spain in the Americas.

As the expedition gathered momentum and more privateers joined, Morgan tasked Collier with leading six ships to Rio de la Hacha to secure provisions, supplies, and intelligence. Collier successfully captured the recently fortified Spanish stronghold there, obtaining much-needed provisions and munitions from the local population.

On October 24, Morgan convened a council of war with his captains and key officers to determine their next target. They debated between Panama, Cartagena de Indias, and Veracruz, all prominent cities in the Gulf of New Spain. Unanimously, they chose Panama, perceived as the most lucrative target due to its immense wealth.

Panama was then the second-largest city in the Western Hemisphere, a bustling hub with over 7,000 households. It played a critical role in the Spanish empire's economy, serving as the transit point for silver from Peruvian mines. This silver was transported overland from Panama to Portobello, where it was loaded onto ships bound for Spain and other Spanish territories.

Morgan's plan required controlling key strategic points. He aimed to capture Providence Island and the Fortress of San Lorenzo on the Chagres River. These locations were crucial for maintaining a supply chain and communication lines. Morgan was familiar with Providence, having captured it before, and knew it harbored Spanish bandits who could be recruited with the promise of payment.

Morgan intended to lead an army of over 1,000 men along the Chagres River, following part of the historic 'Camino de Cruces'—a route the Spanish used to transport goods across the Isthmus of Panama. This route, connecting the Caribbean Sea with the Pacific Ocean, had been successfully navigated by Francis Drake nearly a century earlier.

Morgan also established generous governing articles for the expedition, with captains receiving eight shares, compensation for disability, and bonuses for acts of bravery.

By the end of October, Morgan's fleet had swelled to 30 to 36 English and French ships, including vessels from as far as New England. He commanded the captured French ship Satisfaction, the largest in the fleet, capable of holding eight boats. The fleet included twelve other ships armed with ten or more guns, each carrying an average of seventy-five men, while the remaining ships were smaller, some without any guns.

The size of Morgan's force varied across sources, but it consisted of at least 36 ships with around 2,000 fighting men, excluding mariners and boys. The majority were from the British Isles and its colonies, supplemented by approximately 520 Frenchmen, along with Dutch, free blacks, Native Americans, Portuguese, and a few renegade Spanish.

This privateer army was the largest ever assembled in the Caribbean, well-armed and resolute, a testament to Morgan's leadership and the allure of the potential riches they sought.

In early December, Collier returned to Morgan's fleet with several prisoners. Their confessions indicated that the Spanish were planning an invasion of Jamaica, providing Morgan with further motivation to launch his own offensive.

Around the same time, Morgan received news from Governor Modyford that a peace treaty between England and Spain had been signed in July, though it was still awaiting ratification. Simultaneously, the Spanish, aware of the privateer assembly at Île-à-Vache, were preparing for a potential attack. The general assumption among the Spanish was that Cartagena de Indias would be the target. Consequently, Governor Don Pedro de Ulloa fortified Cartagena, putting the city on high alert. Additionally, other areas along the Spanish Main, including the defenses on the Chagres River organized by the Real Audiencia of Panama under Governor Don Juan Pérez de Guzmán y Gonzaga, were also on guard. Francisco Gonzalez de Salado, Captain of the river, prepared four strong points of high stockades about twenty miles upriver, complete with lookouts and canoe patrols.

Morgan, in response, organized his fleet and set sail from Hispaniola on December 16. He divided his force into two squadrons, now operating under regular commissions as part of Great Britain's naval power. Morgan's main squadron flew the English Red Ensign on the mainmast, symbolizing their allegiance and formal role. The secondary squadron, commanded by Joseph Bradley, flew a White Flag with three small red squares in one corner. Additionally, each ship proudly displayed the Royal standard on her bowsprit, signifying their official capacity and the legitimacy of their mission.

Morgan set his sights on capturing the strategically important islands of Old Providence and the smaller, connected Santa Catalina. He arrived at Providence on December 20th, leading a force of a thousand men through the woods. They encountered minimal resistance and found the island largely deserted.

In contrast, Santa Catalina was heavily fortified, boasting a total of eight fortifications, with Fort San Jerome being the largest. The island was defended by soldiers who were soon faced with Morgan's advancing forces. Morgan, eager to proceed to Panama without delay, resorted to a ruse to coax the Governor into surrendering, threatening to show no mercy if he refused. Surprisingly, the governor capitulated easily but requested a mock attack to maintain a semblance of honor in his surrender. Morgan agreed, seeing it as a way to preserve the lives of both his men and the island's 450 inhabitants, which included 190 soldiers. The spoils from this conquest included 48 cannons, 170 muskets, and over 30,000 pounds of gunpowder. Morgan also released the Spanish prisoners on the island, with three of them agreeing to guide his forces across the Panama Isthmus.

During his time on the island, Morgan was joined by additional privateers, including Colonel Bledry Morgan (no relation), who delivered a letter from Modyford endorsing the expedition. After securing the island, Morgan left a garrison of 130 men, ordering the destruction of all forts except for San Jerome.

To maintain the element of surprise regarding his true objective, Morgan dispatched a detachment of four ships and a boat, led by Captain Joseph Bradley with four hundred men, to capture Fort San Lorenzo on the Río Chagres.

Just four days after leaving Santa Catalina, Captain Joseph Bradley and his four ships approached Fort San Lorenzo, strategically located at the mouth of the Río Chagres. The fort, perched atop a broad mountain and surrounded by rock escarpments, was accessible only from the land side and protected by a drawbridge, casemates, and palisades. The Spanish commander, Don Pedro de Lisardo, had significantly bolstered the fort's defenses, doubling the garrison to 314 men and increasing its artillery to twenty guns.

Upon arrival, the privateers anchored a quarter of a league from the fort at Naranjas Port, launching their initial assault the next morning. This direct frontal attack was repelled by the Spaniards, causing heavy losses among the privateers who only managed to reach the fort's ravine. Undeterred, Bradley ordered a second attack at dusk. Despite facing heavy fire, the privateers managed to launch grenades, igniting several structures within the fort. A stroke of luck occurred when one grenade hit the fort's magazine, causing a massive explosion that threw the defenders into chaos. This allowed the English to breach the fort, resulting in brutal close-quarters combat where no quarter was given. In the fierce fight, Commander Lisardo was killed, refusing to surrender, and eventually, the remaining Spanish forces capitulated.

The aftermath was grim: of the 314 Spanish defenders, only 14 were taken prisoner, while the privateers suffered 30 dead and 160 wounded. Bradley himself was injured in the assault and succumbed to his wounds, along with fifty others. Captain Richard Norman assumed command of the garrison, awaiting Morgan's arrival.

When Morgan reached the fort four days later, the English flag was hoisted high. However, during the approach, four of his ships, including the Satisfaction, ran aground on reefs, leading to the loss of ten men. Morgan salvaged what he could and transferred the resources to the remaining vessels. He spent a week fortifying the fort, utilizing prisoners from Santa Catalina, in anticipation of a possible Spanish counterattack. The fort was garrisoned with 150 men, in addition to another 150 aboard the ships, securing Morgan's line of retreat.

During this period, an English scouting party captured several small Spanish vessels, each armed with two guns. These boats, originally used for cargo transportation along the river, were repurposed to transport many of Morgan's men for the next leg of their journey.

In the early hours, Morgan commenced his ambitious expedition up the Rio Chagres with a formidable force of approximately 1,400 men. This diverse contingent was transported using seven small sailing vessels and thirty-six canoes. Their destination, Panama, lay some fifty miles away, a journey that would require traversing through dense rainforests and swamps, much of it on foot.

The privateers split their approach: nearly half of the troops advanced along the river's edge, while the others navigated by canoe and boat, each group guided through the challenging terrain. On the first day, they covered a significant distance of about eighteen miles, bringing them to Dos Brazos. There, Gonzalez Solado, the captain of the river appointed by the Spanish, had planned an ambush. However, upon realizing the overwhelming numbers of Morgan's force, Solado and his men chose to retreat, destroying everything in their path. As a result, when Morgan's men arrived, they found the area devoid of any valuable resources or provisions.

After spending the night at Dos Brazos, Morgan's troops resumed their journey the next morning, only to encounter increasingly challenging conditions along the river. Due to the dry season, the river's water level had dropped, revealing obstacles like mangrove roots and rotting trees, making navigation difficult. At Cruz du Juan Gallego, the river became too shallow for boats, prompting Morgan to disembark his men. They proceeded overland, carrying the canoes across the remaining part of the isthmus. Morgan left a detachment of 160 men to guard the boats.

As Morgan's force advanced, Don Juan Pérez de Guzmán was kept abreast of their progress. Guzmán hoped that a combination of Spanish ambushes, along with hunger and disease, would halt the privateers. He employed scorched earth tactics, confident that his prepared defenses would stop the English. However, Morgan's guides, leading groups of twenty to thirty men, adeptly navigated potential ambush sites.

Around noon, Morgan's men encountered a challenging swamp with no clear path forward. Despite this, they managed to forge a passage to an area known as Cedro Bueno. The journey was grueling, and with little food available, many of the privateers had not eaten for three to four days. Starvation forced some to resort to eating leaves and other vegetation, with varying degrees of success.

By the next morning, they had reached Barro Colorado. Two canoes sent ahead returned with news of another ambush. Prepared for confrontation, the privateers advanced with war cries, only to find the ambush site, marked by a crescent-shaped palisade of tree posts, abandoned. They took what provisions they could find and burned the rest.

Morgan pressed on despite the lack of food, hacking through the jungle until they reached Torna Munni in the evening. Another planned ambush by the Spanish was abandoned upon their arrival. That night, the men endured cold conditions as they slept along the riverbanks.

The next day, the expedition reached Barbacoa, the first Spanish village and defensive stockade they encountered, only to find it burnt and deserted. With only 216 men, Captain Castillo and his Spanish forces had feared being encircled and retreated. The privateers scoured the village, finding only two sacks of flour, some plantains, and resorting to eating leather bags left behind by the Spanish due to the scarcity of food. By the end of the fifth day, they arrived at another outpost, Torno Marcos, where they anticipated another ambush but found none. They rested there for the night, continuing their arduous journey with dwindling supplies and growing exhaustion.

The privateers resumed their arduous journey, but the toll of hunger and fatigue was evident, with many struggling to continue. Around noon, they reached the village of Venta de Cruces, where they found a house filled with corn and a leather sack of bread, providing much-needed sustenance. During their search, they spotted some natives ahead and gave chase, mistakenly believing they were leading them into a Spanish ambush. The natives, however, crossed the river and evaded capture, while distant Spanish soldiers taunted the privateers. Deciding to remain in Venta de Cruces for the day, the men recuperated.

Leaving Venta de Cruces, the Chagres River turned northeast, prompting the privateers to continue on foot, crossing the river. They left their boats and canoes behind, except for one kept in the village with a small guard, preserving Morgan's line of communication. Panama, now only 25 miles away, became increasingly challenging to reach as the terrain grew mountainous.

Upon reaching the village of Cruz, the privateers found it abandoned and set ablaze, except for the king's shops and stables. Desperate for food, they resorted to killing and eating the dogs housed in the stables. Discovering jars of Peruvian wine, many indulged, leading to bouts of drunkenness and sickness, with some fearing the wine had been poisoned. Morgan, observing the dire state of his men, pondered the feasibility of continuing towards Panama.

The next morning, the path became narrower and steeper, prompting Morgan to select two hundred men to form an advance guard. They navigated through narrow gorges, allowing only two men to pass abreast.

By noon, they arrived at Quebrada Obscural, where Salado had prepared his final ambush, commanding 300 native archers and 100 Spanish musketeers under Captain Joseph de Prado, a survivor from the Fort San Lorenzo. The privateers were caught off guard by a barrage of arrows, resulting in casualties. However, they managed to repel the ambush, with one group of natives holding their ground until their chief was severely wounded.

Despite this setback, the privateers pressed on, and by evening, the dense jungle gave way to open grassland savannah, reducing the risk of ambushes. They found a cluster of houses to rest for the night, gathering their strength to continue their advance the following day.

At dawn, a scouting party from Morgan's forces climbed Ancon Hill. From its summit, they beheld the Pacific Ocean and observed a ship accompanied by five boats leaving Panama. The islands visible in the distance were likely Taboga and Taboguilla. Descending from the hill, the scouts found themselves in a valley teeming with cattle, herded by Spanish horsemen who quickly fled upon noticing the approaching privateers.

The starving privateers seized this opportunity, slaughtering the cattle and horses for a much-needed barbecue feast. After resting and eating for most of the afternoon, they resumed their march and soon glimpsed the roofs and spires of Panama in the distance.

Morgan made camp for the night with his 1,200 men. Meanwhile, the Spanish Governor Don Guzmán, aware of the privateers' arrival, mobilized Panama's defense. The Spanish forces, comprising two cavalry squadrons and four infantry regiments, outnumbered Morgan's men nearly two-to-one. To intimidate the Spanish, Morgan had his men beat drums, blow trumpets, fire volleys, and display flags. Conversely, the Spanish forces were also boosting their morale, with one militiaman reportedly asserting their advantage over the "600 drunkards."

On January 28th, Morgan's men prepared for battle, facing about 1,200 Spanish infantry and 400 cavalry. While the Spanish forces outnumbered Morgan's, many were inexperienced, with only 600 armed with firearms and the rest wielding edged weapons like machetes, pikes, and spears. Governor Guzmán arranged his infantry in a line six men deep, flanked by cavalry units. Behind them, herds of oxen and cattle were poised to be released towards the attackers, potentially disrupting the privateers just as the Spanish infantry engaged.

Morgan arrayed his army just outside cannon range on a plain behind the Matasnillo River, about a mile from the city, with the Spanish positioned on the opposite side. Laurence Prince and John Morris led the main force of around 600 men, while Morgan and Collier commanded the right and left wings.

The battle commenced at 7 pm, with both sides advancing towards each other. Morgan's strategy involved deploying his privateers in four squadrons across the mile-wide plain. He sent a 300-strong contingent, led by Major John Morris, down a ravine towards a small hill on the Spanish right flank. As this squadron disappeared from view, the Spanish front line mistook it for a retreat, prompting them to break rank and pursue aggressively.

Seizing this opportunity, Guzmán ordered the rest of his infantry to advance. However, they were met with intense and organized fire from Morgan's main force, resulting in significant casualties among the Spanish troops. Meanwhile, on the privateers' left flank, led by Laurence Prince, the Spanish cavalry under Francisco Haro charged in. The boggy terrain hindered the cavalry's maneuverability, allowing the privateers to inflict heavy damage with accurate musket fire from a short distance.

The Spanish infantry's attack began to falter, with many soldiers fleeing the battlefield. In the midst of this chaos, the Spanish drovers, panicked by the unfolding events and the gunfire, lost control of the cattle. Guzmán's order to release the cattle only added to the confusion, as many had already been set loose, causing them to stampede over their keepers and Spanish troops. The few cattle that reached the privateer lines were quickly shot by the famished men.

The Spanish forces rapidly disintegrated, with Don Juan Guzmán unsuccessfully attempting to halt the retreat. The battlefield was left in the hands of the English.

The battle, lasting about two hours, was a decisive rout. Spanish casualties were substantial, with estimates of between 400 and 600 dead and wounded. This victory marked a significant triumph for Morgan and his privateers, showcasing their tactical prowess and resilience in the face of a numerically superior force.

Morgan's men relentlessly pursued the fleeing Spanish into Panama City, overcoming resistance at the western bridge and swiftly overpowering barricades set up in the city's main streets. The looting began immediately, with privateers swarming through the city.

Concurrently, fires, likely ordered by Don Juan as a last resort if the city fell, broke out across various quarters, fueled further by the wind. The armoury was also deliberately destroyed, adding to the chaos. The privateers made efforts to extinguish the fires, albeit with limited success. Morgan, aware of the potential risks, forbade his men from drinking discovered Peruvian wine, citing possible poisoning by the inhabitants. This precaution was likely more to prevent his outnumbered force from becoming incapacitated by drunkenness, especially given the possibility of a Spanish counterattack.

Despite Guzmán's efforts to rally his forces, many Spaniards fled to nearby islands or hills, seeking refuge from the conquering privateers.

The day after the victory, Morgan dispatched 180 men to Fort San Lorenzo to announce their triumph. He also ordered the construction of defensive trenches around strategic locations like the Church of the Trinity Fathers, preparing for a potential Spanish counteroffensive. His men then secured the surrounding area, although they were unable to prevent some boats from escaping to nearby beaches.

Further along the coast, the privateers captured a barque that had run aground near La Tasca. Although its crew had attempted to destroy it, the privateers seized it intact, finding it laden with maize, biscuits, sugar, soap, linen, and a significant amount of silver.

Back in Panama City, despite the widespread fires, the privateers discovered hidden treasures. Edward Collier supervised the interrogation of some city residents, and Morgan's fleet surgeon, Richard Browne, later commented on Morgan's fair treatment of the vanquished. The privateers scoured wells, cisterns, and buried caches, uncovering gold and silver objects. They also found shops filled with goods left behind by the fleeing Spaniards, including flour, iron tools, wine, olive oil, and spices - essential supplies for Peru's gold and silver mines.

Morgan organized special units for systematic looting, extending their search up to twenty miles into the mountains. They encountered no resistance and returned with over a hundred mules loaded with loot, money, and more than two hundred prisoners, marking a comprehensive plunder of Panama City.

Upon learning that the Spanish had already transported most of the treasure onto ships, including the 'Santisima Trinidad' under Captain Francisco de Peralta and the 'San Felipe Neri,' which had set sail two days earlier, Morgan directed his efforts towards the nearby islands in Panama Bay. He suspected these islands had become refuges for Spanish citizens and soldiers who fled Panama City.

Morgan had the barque from La Tasca repaired, armed, and placed under the command of Robert Searle. In the following days, this vessel, along with a growing flotilla that included three armed barques and a brigantine, systematically raided and plundered the islands of Perico, Taboga, Taboguila, and other smaller inshore locations. This operation was particularly lucrative, yielding a substantial amount of silver. Many Spanish citizens found hiding on these islands were captured along with their valuables.

By the end of the sacking, Morgan claimed to have taken as many as 3,000 prisoners. He ordered each company to load their share of the plunder onto mules and transport it to Venta de Cruces, planning to use the Río Chagres for their return journey. While much of Panama's wealth was lost in the fires or removed by ships before the privateers' arrival, a significant amount of loot was still amassed.

After spending nearly three weeks in Panama, Morgan and his men prepared for their departure. They had collected a considerable amount of loot, which occupied a substantial amount of space. Meanwhile, Pedro de Castro, the Viceroy of Peru, had been alerted to Morgan's capture of Chagres and his march on Panama. In response, de Castro dispatched an expedition of eighteen ships and nearly 3,000 troops. However, by the time de Castro's forces arrived in Panama, Morgan had already evacuated the city, effectively eluding the Spanish counteroffensive and securing his hard-won treasures.

On February 24th, Morgan's privateers commenced their return journey to Venta de Cruces, laden with treasure on 175 pack animals. Before departing, they spiked the remaining guns and demolished a small fort facing the sea.

During their trek back, the privateers took along approximately 600 prisoners of various ages. Most of these prisoners were ransomed before reaching Chagres, with the prisoner count increasing by another 150 as more stragglers were captured along the way. Upon arriving at Venta de Cruces without any major incidents, Morgan waited for the prisoners' ransom to be delivered, demanding about 150 Pesos per person, with the threat of sending them to Jamaica otherwise. The majority of the ransom was paid, and after nine days, all prisoners were released. During this period, the privateers gathered supplies for their return journey, which proved to be much smoother, especially since the Chagres River was at a suitable level for boat travel all the way to San Lorenzo.

Morgan took the unusual step of ordering his entire army, including himself, to be stripped and searched to ensure that no one was hiding any of the collective loot.

The total value of the treasure amassed during Morgan's expedition was significant, estimated between 140,000 pesos (equivalent to $7 million in modern currency) to 400,000 pesos (about $20 million), excluding the precious stones sold later. Despite the large haul, the prize per man was relatively low due to the size of Morgan's army. After deductions for the wounded, surgeons, carpenters, and officers, the average privateer received about 80 pieces of eight (around $4,000). This modest share led to some discontent and accusations, particularly highlighted in Exquemelin's memoirs, that Morgan had kept the majority of the plunder for himself.

Morgan reached San Lorenzo in just two days via the Chagres. There, he attempted to extort a ransom for the fort as well, but when it became clear that no payment would be made, he ordered the town and its fortifications to be demolished. The French assisted in mining the walls to ensure their complete destruction.

The fleet then set sail for Jamaica, with the French contingent of eight ships returning to Tortuga, while Morgan and four ships, along with about 500 men, headed back to Port Royal. They arrived in early March, only to discover that the peace treaty between Madrid and London had been signed and ratified, marking the end of an era for privateers like Morgan.

As Morgan journeyed from Jamaica, a pivotal moment in history was taking shape. England and Spain, long-time adversaries, had inked the Treaty of Madrid, a pact designed to quell the stormy seas of conflict in the Caribbean. This agreement not only sought peace but also commanded the revocation of all privateering commissions, including Morgan's.

Violet Barbour, a historian, suggests that Spain's insistence on the ousting of Governor Modyford, a key ally of Morgan, might have been a crucial condition of this treaty. The drama heightened as Modyford was arrested and extradited to England by Sir Thomas Lynch, his successor, throwing Jamaica into a whirlwind of change.

The echoes of Morgan's audacious destruction of Panama reverberated through the corridors of power, just as the ink on the treaty was drying. This brazen act plunged England and Spain into a diplomatic crisis, with whispers of war rustling through Europe. To placate the Spanish, England's King Charles II and his Secretary of State, the Earl of Arlington, made a startling move: they ordered the arrest of the famed Captain Morgan.

In April 1672, Morgan found himself in London, not as a prisoner but as a celebrated hero, drawing comparisons to the illustrious Sir Francis Drake. Despite rumors of his imprisonment in the Tower of London, evidence suggests Morgan roamed free in the English capital, his fortunes taking a favorable turn.

Amidst the political chess game, Arlington sought Morgan's expertise in fortifying Jamaica's defenses. Morgan, never officially charged with any crime, provided invaluable insights to the Lords of Trade and Plantations, proving his ignorance of the Treaty of Madrid prior to his attack on Panama.

The winds of change blew yet again in 1674, with John Vaughan, 3rd Earl of Carbery, replacing Lynch in Jamaica, and Morgan appointed as his deputy. Knighted by Charles II, Morgan embarked on a return journey to Jamaica with Carbery and a liberated Modyford, now Jamaica's Chief Justice. Their vessel, laden with armaments to bolster Port Royal's defenses, tragically foundered on the rocks of Île-à-Vache. Stranded but unbroken, Morgan and his crew awaited rescue, their spirits undimmed by the tumultuous seas of fate.

Upon his triumphant return to Jamaica, Captain Henry Morgan was greeted with both reverence and controversy. The Assembly of Jamaica, impressed by his maritime exploits, awarded him a handsome annual salary of £600, recognizing his valuable contributions to the island. This decision, however, sparked tensions with the Earl of Carbery, the governor, who found Morgan's personality and methods disagreeable.

Carbery's displeasure with his deputy was no secret. He openly criticized Morgan's approach to civil governance, lamenting his perceived imprudence and unsuitability for such a role. Further adding to their strained relationship, Carbery expressed his frustration to the Secretary of State about Morgan's indulgences in the lively taverns of Port Royal, notorious for their drinking and gaming.

While Morgan had been tasked with eradicating piracy from the waters around Jamaica, he maintained cordial ties with many privateer captains. He even invested in some of their ventures, navigating the murky waters of legality and diplomacy. With an estimated 1,200 privateers prowling the Caribbean, Port Royal became a bustling haven under Morgan's watchful eye, thriving as long as the privateers paid their dues to him.

Morgan's ability to issue official privateering licenses was curtailed, but his resourcefulness knew no bounds. His brother-in-law, Robert Byndloss, cleverly redirected captains to the French governor of Tortuga for the necessary documents, ensuring Morgan and himself received commissions for each letter issued.

The conflict between Morgan and Carbery escalated in July 1676, with Carbery accusing Morgan before the Assembly of Jamaica of collusion with the French against Spanish interests. Morgan defended himself, insisting that his interactions with French officials were purely diplomatic, not underhanded schemes.

The situation remained unresolved until early 1678, when Carbery was recalled to England, briefly leaving Morgan as the acting governor. In July 1678, Charles Howard, the 1st Earl of Carlisle, was appointed as the new governor.

As the 1670s drew to a close, the rising threat from France in the Caribbean called for decisive action. Morgan, ever the strategist, took the reins of Port Royal's defense. He declared martial law during his temporary governorships in 1678 and 1680, fortifying the town's defenses and significantly bolstering its artillery, showcasing his unwavering commitment to safeguarding Jamaica's shores.

Captain Henry Morgan, once the terror of the seas, found himself navigating the treacherous waters of politics in the Assembly of Jamaica. Alongside his allies, he made valiant efforts to regulate the activities of privateers and pirates. However, Morgan's administration faced internal sabotage when his Secretary, Rowland Powell, deceitfully used his name to issue a proclamation favoring the Royal African Company, contradicting established law and undermining Morgan's authority.

Back in London, Morgan's reputation was further tarnished by two former governors of Jamaica, Carbery and Lynch. Lynch, after making a substantial payment to King Charles II, was reinstated as Jamaica's governor, stripping Morgan of his lieutenant-governor and lieutenant-general titles. Despite this setback, Morgan maintained his seat in the Assembly.

During these tumultuous times, Morgan's long-standing habit of heavy drinking intensified. Disheartened by the loss of his positions and feeling his reputation sullied, he sought solace in alcohol, which took a toll on his health.

Lynch, consolidating his power, systematically removed Morgan's supporters from the Assembly by 1683, and eventually ousted Morgan and his brother-in-law, ensuring the Assembly was filled with his loyalists. Following Lynch's death in 1684, his friend Hender Molesworth temporarily took over as governor.

In 1684, a Dutch book titled "De Americaensche Zee-Roovers" (About the Buccaneers of America) by Exquemelin painted a vivid account of Morgan's exploits. Morgan, determined to protect his reputation, sued the book's publishers, William Crooke and Thomas Malthus, for libel. In court, he vehemently denied any association with piracy, claiming a deep abhorrence for such acts. The court ruled in his favor, retracting the book and awarding him damages.

December 1687 brought a change in Port George with the arrival of Morgan's friend, Christopher Monck, the 2nd Duke of Albemarle. Monck dismissed Molesworth and reinstated Morgan in an advisory role. In July 1688, Albemarle even persuaded the king to allow Morgan to return to the Assembly, but by then, Morgan's health had severely declined.

Albemarle's private physician, Hans Sloane, diagnosed Morgan with dropsy and noticed his excessive drinking. Despite Sloane's advice to cut back on alcohol, Morgan, stubborn and unyielding, continued his habits, a decision that would further deteriorate his health.

During the latter part of the 17th century, Henry Morgan, known for his seafaring exploits, also engaged in confrontations on land as the owner of three large Jamaican plantations. He led three military campaigns against the Maroons of Juan de Serras, a community of runaway slaves who had sought refuge in the Blue Mountains. Despite some initial success, forcing the Maroons to retreat deeper into the mountains, Morgan ultimately failed to capture de Serras or fully subdue the Maroon community.

By the time of his death, Morgan had become a significant plantation owner, holding many African individuals in slavery. His estate, primarily consisting of these plantations, was bequeathed mostly to his wife for her lifetime. After her death, the majority of his land and the enslaved individuals were inherited by his nephew Charles, the second son of Robert Byndloss, who was the Chief Justice of Jamaica in 1681. Additionally, Morgan left a piece of land in the now-defunct parish of St George to another relative, also named Robert Byndloss, the eldest son of his brother-in-law.

Morgan's legacy also extended to his friend, Roger Elletson, to whom he bequeathed land in Saint Mary Parish. This Roger Elletson was an ancestor of a future governor of Jamaica sharing the same name. Morgan's will was executed in 1689, revealing that at the time of his death, he owned 131 African slaves on his estates. This group consisted of 64 males and 67 females, including approximately 33 children. In the context of the era, these individuals were sadly valued as property, with a combined monetary worth of £1,923.

Morgan passed away on August 25, 1688, at Lawrencefield Estate, which is situated in modern-day Port Maria, Jamaica. In honor of his memory, Albemarle arranged a grand state funeral, placing Morgan's body at King's House for the public to pay their respects. To facilitate the participation of pirates and privateers who wished to bid him farewell, an amnesty was declared to ensure they could attend without fear of arrest. His final resting place was Palisadoes cemetery in Port Royal, where a 22-gun salute from the anchored ships in the harbor marked his burial. At the time of his passing, Morgan was a wealthy individual, with a personal fortune valued at £5,263.

Initially, Morgan's will bequeathed his plantations and enslaved individuals to his wife, Mary Elizabeth. However, due to their lack of children, his estate was to be inherited by his nephews, the sons of his brother-in-law Byndloss. The burial of Lady Morgan, his wife, was documented in Saint Andrew Parish, Jamaica, on March 3, 1696.

In his last will, signed on June 17, 1688, Morgan left his Jamaican assets to his godsons Charles Byndloss and Henry Archbold, on the condition that they adopt the Morgan surname. These individuals were the offspring of his two cousins, Anna Petronilla Byndloss and Johanna Archbold. He also allocated an annual sum of £60 from his estate to his sister Catherine Loyd, with the provision that it be paid to "my ever honest cousin Thomas Morgan of Tredegar."

On June 7, 1692, a powerful earthquake struck Port Royal, causing about two-thirds of the town, equivalent to 33 acres (13 ha), to sink into Kingston Harbour shortly after the main tremor. Unfortunately, Palisadoes cemetery, including Morgan's grave, was one of the areas that plunged into the sea during this catastrophe, and his remains have never been recovered since.

William Dampier

William Dampier's life was a remarkable blend of adventure, resilience, and exploration. Born in 1651 at the historic Hymerford House in the picturesque village of East Coker, Somerset, Dampier's early life remains shrouded in some mystery. His baptism took place on September 5th, but the exact date of his birth remains unrecorded. His educational journey began at the prestigious King's School in Bruton, setting the stage for his adventurous life.

Dampier's thirst for exploration and adventure was evident early on. He embarked on his first voyages as a young man, sailing to the distant and rugged coasts of Newfoundland and the exotic lands of Java. These early experiences at sea were just the beginning of what would become a life defined by navigation and discovery.

In 1673, Dampier's life took a significant turn when he joined the Royal Navy. This period was marked by his participation in the intense naval conflicts known as the Battles of Schooneveld, which took place in June of that same year. These battles were pivotal moments in maritime history, and Dampier played his part in them.

However, Dampier's naval career was unexpectedly interrupted by a severe illness, forcing him to return to England for a prolonged period of recuperation. This setback, however, did not dampen his spirit. In the following years, Dampier dabbled in various occupations, from managing plantations in the sun-soaked isles of Jamaica to venturing into the dense forests of Mexico for logging endeavors. Each of these experiences added layers to his already diverse skill set.

Eventually, Dampier's irrepressible draw to the sea led him to join another sailing expedition, a decision that marked the continuation of his life's adventures. Amidst these travels and explorations, Dampier found time for personal life, marrying a woman named Judith around 1679. However, the call of the ocean was too strong to resist, and within a few months of his marriage, he set sail again, leaving his marital life ashore as he pursued his passion for exploration and adventure on the high seas.

In 1679, William Dampier's journey took a thrilling turn as he joined forces with the renowned buccaneer Captain Bartholomew Sharp. Their daring adventures were set against the backdrop of the Spanish Main in Central America. Dampier's seafaring skills were put to the test as they made two voyages to the Bay of Campeche, or "Campeachy" as it was known at the time, located on the northern coast of Mexico. These ventures were the beginning of what would be Dampier's first circumnavigation of the globe.

Dampier's role in this odyssey was far from mundane. He was part of a daring raid across the Isthmus of Darién in Panama, contributing to the capture of Spanish ships in the Pacific. The team's audacity didn't stop there; they went on to raid Spanish settlements in Peru. However, their success waned over time as the Spanish grew more vigilant of their presence. Following an unsuccessful attempt to raid the city of Arica, Dampier, along with a faction of the buccaneers, decided to part ways with the group in April 1681. They trekked back across the Isthmus of Darién, while the rest of their crew continued their journey, eventually navigating around Cape Horn in November of the same year.

Following these exploits, Dampier found himself in Virginia by 1683. Here, he was recruited by privateer John Cooke. Cooke's expedition was ambitious;

they sailed through Cape Horn into the Pacific, spending a year raiding various Spanish territories including Peru, the Galápagos Islands, and Mexico. This expedition was notable for its growth; it amassed a fleet of ten ships at one point. Ambrose Cowley, one of the buccaneers, made significant contributions during this period by producing the first maps of the Galápagos Islands. After Cooke's demise in Mexico, Edward Davis was elected as the new captain, and the ship Batchelor's Delight continued its journey with notable crew members like the future Captain George Raynor.

Dampier's adventure took another twist when he joined the crew of Charles Swan's ship, the Cygnet. On March 31, 1686, they embarked on a bold expedition across the Pacific, targeting the East Indies. Their journey included stops at Guam and Mindanao in the Philippines. The Spanish, viewing the predominantly English crew as pirates, heretics, and even cannibals, were wary of their presence. Eventually, Swan and 36 crew members were left behind in Mindanao, and the remaining privateers, now under Captain John Read, continued their voyage to Manila, Poulo Condor in present-day Vietnam, China, the Spice Islands, and New Holland (now known as Australia). Despite Dampier's later claims of a non-combative role, historical records indicate he was actively involved in piracy, even commanding one of the Spanish ships captured by the Cygnet's crew off Manila in 1687.

On January 5, 1688, the Cygnet, with William Dampier aboard, dropped anchor off the northwest coast of Australia, near King Sound. This marked the beginning of an extended stay in the region, lasting until March 12. During this time, while the ship underwent careening, Dampier diligently recorded observations of the local wildlife, flora, and the indigenous inhabitants. His notes, however, reflected a starkly negative view of the Aboriginal Australians, whom he described in disparaging terms.

Among Dampier's crewmates were several Spanish sailors, one of whom was Alonso Ramírez from San Juan, Puerto Rico. Ramírez's story took a dramatic turn when he was later captured and imprisoned by another pirate, Duncan

Mackintosh, but eventually gained his release.

The year's adventures continued with a drastic turn of events for Dampier and two of his shipmates, who found themselves marooned on one of the Nicobar Islands. In a bid for survival, they fashioned a small canoe, which they initially capsized. After a harrowing experience including surviving a severe storm at sea, they eventually reached Aceh in Sumatra.

Dampier's journey back to England in 1691 was a tale of endurance and survival. He returned via the Cape of Good Hope, destitute, with only his journals and a tattooed slave named Jeoly as his possessions. Jeoly's story was a tragic one; originally from Miangas, he and his mother were captured by slave traders and brought to Mindanao, later falling into the hands of Dampier. Following the death of his mother, Jeoly was consumed by grief. Dampier, despite claiming a close bond with Jeoly in his diaries, sold him to the Blue Boar Inn on Fleet Street in a desperate attempt to recover his financial losses. Jeoly was exhibited to curious crowds as a "prince," only to succumb to smallpox three months later. His life and death sparked numerous fabrications and myths, including the title of "Prince Giolo."

William Dampier, once a buccaneer, experienced a significant shift in his career when he was appointed as the commander of the Roebuck in July 1698. This unusual decision to assign a former pirate to command one of King William's ships can be traced back to Dampier's burgeoning reputation, which he had enhanced through his extensive travels and the public exhibition of the tattooed Prince Jeoly and his mother. Acquired during his first circumnavigation, Jeoly and his mother had become known as a "just wonder of the age," as described in a broadsheet from 1691–1692. Dampier's fame was not just limited to the public; his 1697 publication, "A New Voyage Round the World," had garnered him recognition and respect from a wide range of influential figures, including academics, seafarers, politicians, and even royalty.

Dampier's connections with prominent individuals of the time are highlighted by an entry from the diary of John Evelyn, dated August 16, 1698. Evelyn noted a dining encounter with Samuel Pepys, a notable naval administrator, where Dampier was present. He described Dampier as a former buccaneer who had brought the painted Prince Job (Jeoly) to England and published an account of his extraordinary adventures. Despite his notorious past, Dampier was described by Evelyn as surprisingly modest, especially considering the company he had kept. This meeting took place at a time when Dampier was preparing for another expedition, encouraged and supported by the king, who had provided a ship of 290 tons for his journey.

The Roebuck, mentioned in Evelyn's diary, was chosen as a replacement for the Jolly Prize, which Dampier found inadequate for his ambitious plans. His intention was to search for Terra Australis and to explore the uncharted eastern coast of New Holland (Australia) via the perilous route of Cape Horn. This decision underscored Dampier's boldness and his desire to push the boundaries of contemporary navigation and exploration.

Setting sail from England on January 14th, Dampier intended to take the Cape Horn route but was delayed, leading him to opt for the Cape of Good Hope instead. During the journey, a tense and tumultuous relationship developed between Dampier and his first lieutenant, George Fisher. Their interactions, characterized by a lack of dignity and self-respect, oscillated between periods of drinking together and bouts of personal abuse and even physical confrontations in front of the crew. This volatile atmosphere culminated in Dampier caning Fisher, restraining him in irons, and eventually confining him to his quarters. The crew was sharply divided over this matter, and fearing a mutiny, Dampier decided to disembark Fisher at Bahia in Brazil, where he was temporarily imprisoned before returning to England.

While at the Cape of Good Hope, Dampier was perplexed by the unusual variations in compass readings. He recorded his observations, noting his confusion and shock at these anomalies. This attention to detail in his navigational observations was later commended by Admiral William Henry Smyth. Smyth recognized Dampier as one of the first seamen to contribute to the study of local magnetic attraction, noting that his findings at the Cape of Good Hope inspired the esteemed navigator Matthew Flinders to further investigate this phenomenon.

After departing from the Cape of Good Hope, Dampier made his first landing on the Australian continent in August 1699 at what he named Shark Bay in Western Australia. His explorations extended to Lagrange Bay, near modern-day Broome in Roebuck Bay. Here, Dampier meticulously documented and collected a variety of natural specimens, including shells, which later earned him the accolade of "Australia's first natural historian."

In November, following a stop at Timor, Dampier reached the northwest cape of New Guinea, near the current Selat Dampier in West Papua. He dispatched his crew to a nearby "small woody island," which he named Cockle Island, where they gathered numerous giant clam shells. The crew then navigated around the northern part of New Guinea, bestowing the name Nova Britannia upon the region. The strait they traversed between these two islands was later named the Dampier Strait in honor of Dampier's contributions to exploration and navigation.

William Dampier's ambitious plans to explore the eastern coast of Australia in 1700 were thwarted by the deteriorating condition of his ship, the Roebuck, which was being ravaged by shipworms. Reluctantly, Dampier abandoned his exploration efforts, leaving the task to be later undertaken by Lieutenant James Cook more than fifty years afterward. Instead, Dampier redirected his voyage into the Indian Ocean, seeking the Tryal Rocks, infamous for the wreck of the English East India Company ship Tryall in 1622, the first recorded European shipwreck on the Australian coast.

However, the Roebuck's severe leakage made the search for the Tryal Rocks unsustainable, prompting Dampier to sail towards Batavia (present-day

Jakarta), the hub of the Dutch East India Company's extensive trade network. Despite managing some repairs in Batavia, the ship's condition remained precarious as they journeyed back towards the Cape of Good Hope, arriving there by the end of December.

In mid-January 1701, the Roebuck departed the Cape of Good Hope, stopping at St Helena until February 13. They then sailed towards Ascension Island, sighting it on February 21. Tragically, the ship developed a critical leak, proving impossible to repair. The crew was forced to run the ship towards the shore, anchoring in shallow waters. After moving some essential items, including Dampier's journals and specimens, to safety, the crew abandoned the sinking Roebuck.

Miraculously, on April 8, four East India Company ships arrived at the bay and rescued Dampier and his crew. The Hastings, one of the rescuing ships, managed to recover an anchor and cable from the Roebuck but lost a grappling anchor in the process. These ships transported Dampier and his crew back to England, where in 1703, he published "A Voyage to New Holland," which was well-received and further enhanced his reputation as an explorer.

Despite the acclaim, Dampier faced criticism at a court martial for his ship's loss and his treatment of George Fisher, which tarnished his prospects for official patronage. However, Dampier's contributions to science continued to be significant. The plant collections salvaged from the wreck were donated to the Royal Society and eventually found their way to the University of Oxford.

In 1701, as the War of the Spanish Succession raged, English privateering efforts were ramped up against French and Spanish targets. William Dampier was appointed to lead the 26-gun ship St George, manned by a crew of 120. Alongside them was the 16-gun Cinque Ports, with 63 men. They embarked on their mission from Kinsale, Ireland, on September 11, 1703. Their voyage around Cape Horn was marked by treacherous storms, eventually leading them to the Juan Fernández Islands off Chile's coast in February 1704. There, they encountered a heavily armed French merchant ship. A fierce seven-hour battle ensued, but Dampier and his crew were ultimately repelled.

Dampier's journey along the Peruvian coast involved capturing several smaller Spanish ships. However, he released them after taking only portions of their cargoes, citing their potential interference with his larger ambitions. These ambitions were centered around a planned raid on Santa María, a town on the Gulf of Panama rumored to hold significant gold reserves from nearby mines. The raid, however, was met with unexpectedly strong resistance, forcing Dampier and his men to retreat.

In a dramatic turn of events, the Cinque Ports, separated from St George in May 1704, eventually sank off what is now Colombia after marooning Alexander Selkirk on an island due to his complaints about the ship's condition. Some crew members survived the shipwreck but were captured by the Spanish.

The remaining goal for St George was to intercept and capture the Manila galleon, the primary target of the expedition. In December 1704, they spotted what was likely the Nuestra Señora del Rosario. The galleon, initially caught off guard, managed to ready its formidable armaments while Dampier's crew debated their attack strategy. Outgunned by the galleon's heavy artillery, St George sustained significant damage and had to withdraw.

This failed engagement signaled the disintegration of the expedition. Dampier, with about thirty men, remained on the damaged St George, while the rest commandeered a captured barque and sailed to Amboyna in the Dutch East Indies. The St George, beyond repair and beset by shipworms, was abandoned on the coast of Peru. Dampier and his remaining crew, taking a Spanish prize ship to the East Indies, were initially imprisoned as pirates by the Dutch but were subsequently released.

By the end of 1707, Dampier, now shipless, managed to return to England, marking the end of a tumultuous and challenging phase in his maritime career.

In 1708, William Dampier took on a new role aboard the privateer Duke, not as its captain, but as a pilot. The Duke, along with its consort ship, Duchess, navigated through the treacherous waters around Cape Horn into the South Pacific Ocean. This expedition, commanded by Woodes Rogers, proved to be significantly more successful than Dampier's previous ventures. A highlight of this voyage was the rescue of Alexander Selkirk on February 2, 1709. Selkirk had been marooned for several years and his story later inspired the classic novel "Robinson Crusoe." The expedition was financially lucrative, amassing plunder valued at £147,975, equivalent to about £23.4 million in today's money. This fortune was largely due to the capture of the Spanish galleon Nuestra Señora de la Encarnación y Desengaño off the coast of Mexico in December 1709.

In January 1710, Dampier crossed the Pacific Ocean aboard the Duke, in the company of the Duchess and two captured prize ships. They made a stop at Guam before reaching Batavia. After a refit at Horn Island near Batavia and selling one of the prize ships, the expedition headed for the Cape of Good Hope, where they spent over three months waiting for a convoy. Leaving the Cape in the company of other English ships, Dampier served as the sailing master of the captured Encarnación.

The expedition eventually returned to London, anchoring in the Thames on October 14, 1711, after further delays at the Texel. However, Dampier's personal fortunes at the end of his life were not as grand as his maritime exploits. He passed away in the Parish of St Stephen Coleman Street in London, with the exact date, circumstances of his death, and his final resting place remaining unknown. It is speculated that he might have been buried in St Stephen's Church, but this cannot be confirmed as the church was destroyed during bombing in 1940. Dampier's will was proven on March 23, 1715, suggesting he likely died earlier in the month, although this is not definitively known. At the time of his death, his estate was burdened with almost £2,000 in debt.

176

François l'Olonnais

François L'Olonais, birth name Jean-David Nau, was a notorious figure in the annals of piracy, whose life story reads like a script from a swashbuckling adventure. Born around 1630 in the scenic coastal town of Les Sables-d'Olonne, France, he was destined for a life marked by the high seas and high stakes. In his early twenties, Nau, driven by a spirit of adventure or perhaps a sense of desperation, found himself in the Caribbean. There, he initially endured the grueling life of an indentured servant on a plantation. This experience, far from breaking his spirit, seemed to forge it anew.

After three years, Nau's path took a dramatic turn as he joined the rugged band of hunters on Hispaniola. These men, who smoked their meat on traditional grills, were dubbed 'buccaneers', a term that would soon become synonymous with piracy. The buccaneers, constantly harassed by the Spanish authorities, developed a fierce resilience, often retreating into the island's untamed interior to escape persecution. It was in this crucible of resistance and defiance that Nau transformed into François L'Olonais, the pirate.

L'Olonais's career as a pirate was marked by extraordinary feats and terrifying cruelty. Operating from the pirate haven of Tortuga, he became a scourge on the Spanish Main. His most infamous exploit was the 1667 attack on Venezuela, where his brutal methods earned him the chilling moniker 'Flail of the Spanish'. His reign of terror continued unabated across the Caribbean, particularly in the Bay of Honduras.

However, L'Olonais's tale, filled with plunder and peril, met a grim end. In a twist of fate, this feared pirate met his demise at the hands of local cannibals, who butchered and consumed him. His life, a vivid tableau of piracy's golden age, remains a captivating chapter in the history of the Caribbean.

The story of Tortuga, or Ile de la Tortue, weaves a captivating tapestry of piracy and colonial intrigue. Nestled in the northwest of Hispaniola, a land now divided into Haiti and the Dominican Republic, Tortuga emerged in the 1630s as a crucial stronghold for buccaneers. Its name, inspired by its turtle-like shape when viewed from the sea, hinted at the unique character of this island.

During this tumultuous era, the French colonial powers in Saint Domingue, located on the opposite side of Hispaniola, played a subtle game of politics and power. They maintained a tacit alliance with the buccaneers of Tortuga, seeing them as a convenient buffer against the relentless incursions of Spanish warships. This arrangement allowed Tortuga to flourish as a pirate haven, a place where lawlessness and freedom intertwined.

Enter François L'Olonais, a figure who would become synonymous with the darkest aspects of buccaneering. Arriving in Tortuga in the 1660s, L'Olonais quickly established himself as a force to be reckoned with. The governor of the island, recognizing his ruthless efficiency, gifted him a captured ship, effectively sanctioning his piratical raids against the Spanish.

L'Olonais's notoriety was cemented by his unparalleled cruelty. Among the ranks of buccaneers, a group hardly known for their gentleness, L'Olonais stood out as the most depraved and merciless. His preferred method of dealing with captives was execution, often by beheading. This grim practice was vividly captured in Alexander Exquemelin's "The Buccaneers of America," a sensational account published in English in 1684. The book, teeming with exaggerated and lurid tales, painted L'Olonais as a madman of grotesque proportions.

One particularly chilling episode encapsulates L'Olonais's savage reputation. In a display of unspeakable brutality, he is said to have cut out the heart of a captive, taken a bite from it, and then, in a macabre gesture, stuffed it into the mouth of another horrified prisoner. Such acts of savagery earned him the chilling epithet 'Flail of the Spanish'.

Ironically, L'Olonais's brutal treatment of his captives backfired. Spanish settlers and crew members, aware of his reputation, preferred to fight to the death rather than face the gruesome fate that awaited them upon capture. This unyielding resistance added yet another layer of bloodshed to L'Olonais's already violent campaign.

The life of François L'Olonais was marked by a series of violent encounters, some of which saw him on the defensive. A particularly harrowing incident occurred when his ship met disaster on the Campeche coast of Mexico. There, L'Olonais and his crew faced the wrath of a local indigenous tribe. In a brutal clash, the majority of his men were mercilessly slain. L'Olonais, however, demonstrated his cunning and survival instincts in this dire situation. He resorted to a macabre but effective tactic: covering himself in the blood of his fallen comrades and playing dead among their bodies. This gruesome act of deception allowed him to evade the fate that befell his crew.

The buccaneer's resourcefulness did not end there. From the clutches of near-certain death, he managed to find his way back to the relative safety of Tortuga, commandeering a stolen canoe to navigate his way back to his base. This escape and return were testament to L'Olonais's tenacity and resilience in the face of adversity.

Despite this brush with death, L'Olonais remained unshaken in his ruthless approach. In a bold move, he attacked a warship anchored in a Cuban port, capturing several Spaniards in the process. True to his merciless reputation, he beheaded all but one of his captives. The spared prisoner was tasked with delivering a chilling message to the governor of Havana: L'Olonais declared, through this missive, his unyielding intent to show no mercy to any Spaniards he captured. This episode was not just a display of his brutal tactics but also served as a psychological warfare against the Spanish authorities.

The captured warship became a new tool in L'Olonais's arsenal. He commandeered it for his own use, adding to his capability to wreak havoc. With this reinforced firepower, he set his sights on the waters off the coast of Venezuela, continuing his reign of terror on the Spanish Main.

The era of privateering buccaneers was a time of blurred lines between sanctioned naval warfare and outright piracy. While these buccaneers were officially authorized by their colonial governments to target Spanish ships, they often extended their activities to include assaults on ports, especially during times of war. This was the backdrop for François L'Olonais's infamous raid on the Venezuelan coast in 1667, set against the backdrop of the Franco-Spanish War (1667-1668). This conflict provided a veneer of legitimacy to L'Olonais's actions, as it made the Spanish territories fair game for French privateers.

L'Olonais, leading a formidable force of 600 men and eight ships, was a fearsome sight. His crew, a mix of hardened French buccaneers from Hispaniola and Tortuga, were well-equipped for their mission. Before even reaching Venezuelan shores, they had already captured two Spanish ships, seizing a bounty of silver, gems, muskets, gunpowder, and cacao. Their primary target was Maracaibo, a bustling settlement of about 4,000 inhabitants and a hub for the lucrative pearl trade. The buccaneers' strategic brilliance shone through as they attacked the port's fortifications from the land, bypassing the 16 cannons aimed seaward, and easily overpowered the defenses.

Upon entering Maracaibo, L'Olonais and his men found the town nearly deserted. The residents, anticipating the raid, had fled, taking most of their valuables with them. Undeterred, L'Olonais dispatched his men into the surrounding woods for two weeks to hunt down the hiding inhabitants. This ruthless search resulted in the capture and brutal torture of 20 Spaniards, who were then summarily executed.

The buccaneers' next target was Gibraltar, located on the opposite side of Lake Maracaibo. Here, they faced a more formidable challenge. The garrison, equipped with eight cannons, mounted a valiant defense, inflicting significant casualties on the buccaneers. Despite their losses, L'Olonais's men eventually overcame the resistance, leaving 200 defenders dead and taking 150 prisoners. During their four-week occupation, they amassed more loot and subjected the local population to a reign of terror.

In a typical buccaneer fashion, L'Olonais threatened to burn down Gibraltar unless a ransom was paid. The besieged residents managed to scrape together 10,000 silver pesos, a significant sum, to spare their town from destruction. Not satisfied with this, the buccaneers returned to Maracaibo and extorted an even larger ransom from the Spanish authorities, amounting to 30,000 pieces of eight.

Triumphant, L'Olonais and his crew returned to Tortuga, laden with their ill-gotten gains. The pirates indulged in a debauched spree of wine, women, and gambling, squandering their wealth within three weeks. But the call of the sea was relentless. As their funds dwindled, L'Olonais and his men were once again drawn to the allure of the open waters, ready for their next adventure in piracy.

François L'Olonais's life as a buccaneer was a series of daring raids and audacious exploits, and his next venture was no less bold. Setting his sights on the coast of Nicaragua, L'Olonais gathered an impressive force of 700 men and six ships, ready to once again challenge Spanish dominion in the Americas. This expedition, aimed at raiding Spanish possessions, was a testament to his relentless pursuit of plunder and adventure.

However, this endeavor was fraught with challenges from the outset. As the fleet made its way, it was becalmed in the Gulf of Honduras, a setback that might have discouraged a lesser pirate. But L'Olonais was undeterred. Undaunted by the change in plans, the buccaneers redirected their attention to the Honduran coast, setting their sights on the small settlement of Puerto Caballos. True to their fearsome reputation, the arrival of L'Olonais's fleet sent the locals fleeing, leaving behind only the unfortunate few who couldn't escape. These captives faced the grim fate of torture, as the buccaneers sought information on hidden valuables.

The raid, however, yielded little success. Even a Spanish ship they captured turned out to be a disappointment, its hold empty. An inland expedition only led to an ambush by a Spanish force, and the capture of San Pedro, a tiny settlement, offered no valuable loot. This series of misfortunes culminated in a failed enterprise, leading to disillusionment among L'Olonais's ranks, with many of his captains deserting the expedition.

L'Olonais's notorious career, marked by cruelty and violence, was destined for a grim end. In 1668, as he navigated towards Panama, he and his crew captured a Spanish galleon. Unfamiliar with handling such a heavy and cumbersome vessel, they lost control in the challenging waters and ran aground on the Mosquito Coast of Nicaragua. Forced to improvise, L'Olonais had his crew begin constructing rudimentary boats. During a foraging expedition inland, he narrowly escaped a confrontation with a Spanish force.

Continuing their journey down the coast, L'Olonais's luck finally ran out in the Gulf of Darien. In a twist of fate mirroring his own brutal methods, he was captured by local cannibals. In a macabre end to a life marked by bloodshed, L'Olonais was subjected to a slow and torturous death. Piece by piece, he was cut apart, roasted, and consumed. The remnants of this feared pirate were reduced to ashes and scattered to the winds, closing the final chapter of one of the most feared buccaneers in history. His demise, as brutal as his life, served as a stark reminder of the perilous and unforgiving world of piracy in the Caribbean.

Bibliography

Allen, H. R. Buccaneer: Admiral Sir Henry Morgan. Arthur Baker, 1976.

Andrade, Tonio. "The Company's Chinese Pirates: How the Dutch East India Company Tried to Lead a Coalition of Pirates to War against China, 1621-1662." 2004.

Bak, Greg. Barbary Pirate: The Life and Crimes of John Ward, the Most Infamous Privateer of His Times. Sutton Publishing Ltd, 2006.

Beer, Anna. Patriot or Traitor: The Life and Death of Sir Walter Ralegh. Oneworld, 2018.

Bevan, Bryan. The Great Seamen of Elizabeth I. Robert Hale, 1971.

Breverton, Terry. Admiral Sir Henry Morgan: The Greatest Buccaneer of them all. Glyndŵr Publishing, 2005.

Chin, James K. "Merchants, Smugglers, and Pirates: Multinational Clandestine Trade on the South China Coast, 1520–50." 2010.

Clulow, Adam. "The Pirate and the Warlord." Journal of Early Modern History, 2012.

Curzon, Catherine. "Grace O'Malley, the Fearless 16th-Century Irish Pirate Queen Who Stood Up to the English." Mental Floss, 30 January 2019, https://www.mentalfloss.com/article/571511/grace-omalley-pirate-queen.

Dolin, Eric Jay. Black Flags, Blue Waters: The Epic History of America's Most Notorious Pirates. Liveright, 2018.

Dwyer, Jack. Dorset Pioneers. The History Press, 2009.

Gill, Anton. The Devil's Mariner: A Life of William Dampier, Pirate and Explorer, 1651–1715. Michael Joseph, 1997.

Howgego, Raymond John, editor. "Cavendish, Thomas." Encyclopedia of Exploration to 1800. Hordern House, 2003.

Kelsey, Harry. Sir John Hawkins, Queen Elizabeth's Slave Trader. Yale

University Press, 2003.

Lyon, Eugene. The Enterprise of Florida: Pedro Menéndez de Avilés and the Spanish Conquest of 1565–1568. University Press of Florida, 1983.

Marley, David. Pirates of the Americas. ABC-CLIO, 2010.

Quinn, David B. Explorers and Colonies: America, 1500-1625. Hambleton Press, 1990.

Sugden, John. Sir Francis Drake. Barrie & Jenkins, 1990.

www.ingramcontent.com/pod-product-compliance
Lightning Source LLC
Chambersburg PA
CBHW071613150726
48000CB00004B/1709